Parsonage in a Pear Tree

Lighthearted Glimpses at Life in a Small Town Pastor's Family

Arlo T. Janssen

Copyright © 2009 by Arlo T. Janssen.

Library of Congress Control Number: 2008911448
ISBN: Hardcover 978-1-4363-9161-0
Softcover 978-1-4363-9160-3

All rights reserved. No part of this book may be reproduced or transmitted in any form or by any means, electronic or mechanical, including photocopying, recording, or by any information storage and retrieval system, without permission in writing from the copyright owner.

This book was printed in the United States of America.

To order additional copies of this book, contact:
Xlibris Corporation
1-888-795-4274
www.Xlibris.com
Orders@Xlibris.com
47887

CONTENTS

Prologue: What Is A Parsonage In A Pear Tree? 11

Chapter One: As For Me And My House,
   We Will Serve The Lord. 15
Chapter Two: Where There's Smoke, There's Fire In
   Dad's Eyes! 24
Chapter Three: Ducks In The Parsonage Yard? 28
Chapter Four: Christmas At The Parsonage 34
Chapter Five: Bath In A Snowstorm? 42
Chapter Six: Sliding On The Hills In Odessa 47
Chapter Seven: Ice Skating In And Near Odessa 53
Chapter Eight: God Provides; That's All There Is To It! ... 58
Chapter Nine: Farmed Out As A Child 63
Chapter Ten: Will Our Pup Be Waiting For Us In Heaven? ... 70
Chapter Eleven: Jay Gould's Carnival Comes To Odessa! ... 77
Chapter Twelve: The Bride And Groom Just *Disappeared!* ... 83
Chapter Thirteen: My First Bike—a Two-dollar Investment ... 88
Chapter Fourteen: My Most Humiliating Moment 93
Chapter Fifteen: Twenty Years Of Janssens In
   The Odessa School 98
Chapter Sixteen: Collecting Little Windows Of History
   (Postage Stamps) 105

Chapter Seventeen: Ruth And Ihno—the Firstborn
Janssens 111
Chapter Eighteen: Pool Spells "T-r-o-u-b-l-e" 123
Chapter Nineteen: Summer Evenings In Odessa Before TV 128
Chapter Twenty: Missionfests In Odessa And Yellow Bank.... 134
Chapter Twenty-one: Play Of Children In Odessa
In The '30s And '40s 158
Chapter Twenty-two: As A Kid, I Learned
About Gambling! 165
Chapter Twenty-three: Halloween In Odessa, Awhile Ago! 172
Chapter Twenty-four: First, We Washed Off At The River 177
Chapter Twenty-five: A Fourth Of July When Fun Turned
To Tragedy For A Brother Who Never Lost
His Spirit! 181
Chapter Twenty-six: Our Father, The *Sehlsorger*
(Carer Of Souls).. 188
Chapter Twenty-seven: Cotton Blossom Singers At
Trinity Church 197
Chapter Twenty-eight: My Special Fourth Of July 202
Chapter Twenty-nine: Summer Bible School In Odessa
And Yellow Bank 208
Chapter Thirty: How Well I Remember December 7, 1941! 214
Chapter Thirty-one: Farm Work Is Best Done By Farmers..... 221
Chapter Thirty-two: Journey To Stromers' In 1939 229
Chapter Thirty-three: Snowstorms On The Plains
Of Minnesota 240
Chapter Thirty-four: Baseball In Odessa During
World War II 250

Chapter Thirty-five: My Job As Church Janitor 257

Chapter Thirty-six: Our Mother, A Gift From God For Us And For Dad 263

Chapter Thirty-seven: Runaway Horses 276

Chapter Thirty-eight: Movies In Our Life When We Were Kids 281

Chapter Thirty-nine: Teaching In A One-room School While Still Growing Up (In More Ways Than One) 287

Chapter Forty: Beginning To Prepare For The Ministry As A Young Boy 292

Chapter Forty-one: Wandering The Streets Of Odessa At Age Seventy-five...299

Epilogue: It Was All Worthwhile, And I Thank God For It. 313

TO MY WIFE, OFELIA, MY BEST FRIEND
AND THE JOY OF MY LIFE

SPECIAL THANKS TO **JERRY WHITE,** A COMPUTER MENTOR LIKE NO OTHER AND to Jerry's wife, **Sandy,** and my wife, **Ofelia,** for their patience, love, and understanding.

PROLOGUE

WHAT IS A PARSONAGE IN A PEAR TREE?

Was there ever such a thing as a *parsonage in a pear tree?* Not really, I'm sure, but we used that phrase frequently, for the fun of it, when we sang the "Twelve Days of Christmas" at our house—Trinity Lutheran Parsonage—in Odessa, Minnesota. Our large family lived in that house next to the church for over twenty years from 1927 to 1947.

There was *a lot of singing* in the house we called home during those years, and there was *a lot of laughing* too. It was common for us to change words to some songs *as a joke*. It just sounded humorous to us to sing, and *"a parsonage* in a pear tree," instead of *a partridge.*

It's been said that *living in a parsonage is like living in a fishbowl.* Our mother, who herself was the daughter of a pastor, said she did not feel as though life in a parsonage was like that. Of course, her father, the Reverend Theodore Thormaehlen, did not seem to be bothered so much about what people thought of the pastor's family or their life. He was a rather intellectual person, who kept pretty much to himself most of the time.

Our father, on the other hand, was very much of a *people person*, so he was more aware of what the parishioners thought. In fact, we heard him say many times, "Was werden die Leute sagen?" (What will the people say?) He knew well that folks, especially in a small town, paid a lot of attention to what others were doing, the pastor's family in particular.

We often joked, saying, "In a town like Odessa, if you don't know what you are doing, ask your neighbor. He'll know."

Seriously, some people in a small town seem to make it their business to know what others are doing. That is sometimes a good thing because many people are very helpful in time of need. It can be a negative thing though, too, when people get their nose into things they shouldn't.

It has been said that *it takes a village to raise a child*. Likewise, a congregation can help in ways to bring up the pastor's children. However, it can again be a negative when people are too adversely critical because they expect too much of *the preacher's kids*.

It may be natural for parishioners to hold *their pastor* to a certain standard. Sometimes, however, they place the pastor on too high a pedestal, almost as though they expect him to be *without sin*. And unfortunately, some hold the pastor's children to the same high standard.

Children are children, however, and should be judged as such. I can tell you for sure, *all in our family were human!*

If I had majored in psychology, I think I would like to have done a dissertation on *pastors' children.* I'm sure that a study of that kind would show that some pastors' children *go wrong,* in a sense, because they have been held to an unrealistic standard. They rebel, it seems, to prove that they can do *what they want to.*

On the other side of the coin, when pastor's children do what is good and right, frequently they are not given any credit. "After all," it seems some people think, "they should not be praised for doing what is expected of them."

This book is not a study of pastors' children—not anything like it. Therefore, *I now want to tell you what a blessing it can also be to be brought in a parsonage, especially if the pastor and his wife are very committed, loving, and caring Christians, such as our parents were.*

Our parents were not perfect, but they were very committed Christians, and it is my opinion that they brought us up quite well. We were taught that *Christians are saints only in the righteousness of Christ.* And as saints in Christ, our life was to be *a striving* to live according to the commandments of God, *in appreciation for God's making us His own.* We were not trying to earn our way to heaven, but rather saying *thank you* to the Lord.

We were taught also that *God forgives,* and we were assured that *God's forgiveness is the greatest gift we could possibly receive,* for it even makes it possible for us to be *with the Lord in heaven, after this life*!

This book is not a biography of our family. It is, rather, a series of episodes *primarily from my life, number 7 of the ten children born to our parents*—the first of the siblings born in Odessa.

I've written forty-one episodes for this book. They evolved from voluminous notes I kept since grade school and from rather vivid memories. Also, as you, friends and relatives, know, stories of our experiences have been told and retold many times.

It is my hope that you will enjoy reading about my growing up in a village parsonage as much as I have enjoyed writing about it. *I wouldn't have traded anything for where and how I was brought up.* I hope that is apparent to you as you read on.

CHAPTER ONE

AS FOR ME AND MY HOUSE, WE WILL SERVE THE LORD.
—Joshua 24:15

Odessa, the village in which I was born and grew up, is seven miles southeast of Ortonville, about five miles (as the crow flies) from the border of South Dakota. The nearest of the ten thousand lakes in Minnesota to Odessa is Lake Big Stone, about seven miles away. That lake's other claim to fame is that it is the source of the Minnesota River.

Today Odessa has only a little over one hundred people and only a few businesses. Though the village was not much bigger in my growing up years, that small spot in Minnesota *was my* world!

When I grew up in Odessa, in the 1930s and early '40s, there were about three hundred people in the village. There certainly must have been at least that many cats and dogs too as well as a few cows, horses, and goats.

I'm sure that more than a hundred farm families in the vicinity received mail through the Odessa Post Office rural delivery system. Also, most of those farmers did their basic business, both buying and selling, in the village of Odessa at that time.

Today there aren't nearly as many farm families in the vicinity. The reason for that is not only that many people have left farms for city life, but also, the farms are much larger today. There are therefore fewer people living on farms and operating them. The technology today makes it possible for more farming to be done by fewer people.

In the thirties and forties, there were perhaps 40 percent of the people in the United States living on farms, making their living from the land. Today, at the beginning of the twenty-first century, it's 3 percent.

Incidentally, because of modern technology, the 3 percent produce more than the 40 percent did six decades ago.

The village of Odessa, Minnesota, is typical of so many little towns in the United States; there is simply less of a sociological reason for the town to exist today compared with years ago.

When I grew up there, Odessa was a bustling little town with about forty businesses, if I counted accurately. *Today (in 2008) there are, I believe, four.*

The town also had an elementary and a high school, although all twelve grades used the same building. Many families were large, though not all were as large as ours. We were ten children. Nine grew up of the ten, and most of us did our growing up in the village of Odessa and went to school there.

The first six of the children in our family were born in Wisconsin, but they ranged in age from one to ten years old when the family came to Odessa, so they did most of their growing up in Odessa.

Odessa Public School (District 24), with its twelve grades, was not without Janssens from 1927 to 1947. When the family arrived in Odessa in 1927, there were already three of school-age. When the family left Odessa in 1947, there was still one in school. The rest of us were in the Odessa school between those years.

I attended the Odessa school for ten years, from 1934 to 1944, from first grade through my sophomore year of high school. I graduated from high school at Concordia Academy in St. Paul in 1946.

The village of Odessa today is fairly quiet. In the thirties and early forties, though only a small village, it was very much *alive,* particularly on Wednesdays and Saturdays—the special trading days at the nearly forty businesses.

Some of the establishments at that time which I recall, were the following: *two grain elevators, a lumber and coal yard, three grocery stores, a meat market, two creameries and poultry shops, two hardware stores, a farm implement business, two blacksmiths, and a harness shop.*

In addition to that, there *were two gas stations, an auto repair garage, a small hotel, two barbershops, a pool hall, a shoe repair shop, even an ice cream parlor, and several watering holes (bars).*

There were also *two thriving granite quarries, Cold Spring and Delano, near the village.* Most of the quarry workers lived in or near Odessa.

In the town, there *were also two churches: Lutheran* (of which our father was pastor) and *the Evangelical Reformed Church.* Trinity, the congregation with a church next to our house, was made up largely of German families. Many of them spoke German, and especially the older folks preferred to use German in their spiritual life.

I was born in the parsonage of Trinity Lutheran Church, Dr. Shelver from nearby Ortonville "officiating" at my birth at home. My father, the Reverend Ihno Janssen Sr. was the pastor of Trinity Church from 1927 to 1947. Born October 1, 1928, I was the seventh Janssen child, the first of the family born in Odessa.

The first six children were born where our pastor father served parishes at Milan and Mattoon, Wisconsin, from 1915 to 1927. Ruth, Ihno Junior, and Anita were born in Milan, near Wausau; Adelheid, Vernon, and Marcia were born in Mattoon, about fifty miles from Green Bay, in northeast Wisconsin.

Northeast Wisconsin was also where our parents met, in a community called Pine River, between Merrill and Anitgo. Dad came to live in Pine River, near Merrill, when he immigrated to the United States in 1907 from Germany. Our mother's father was the pastor of the Lutheran Church in Pine River where our parents met.

Minnie Thomaehlen helped Dad learn English in Wisconsin when she was fourteen, and he was twenty. They were married, however, in Yellow Bank Township, Minnesota, six miles southeast of Ortonville, in 1916, when she was twenty-two and he twenty-eight.

Mother's father, the Reverend Theodore Thormaehlen, had come to serve Immanuel Lutheran Church in Yellow Bank a few years after Mom and Dad had met in Wisconsin. Pastor Thormaehlen served the church at Yellow Bank from 1911 to 1928.

My parents gave me, their seventh child, the name *Arlo,* which has caused me a few interesting problems now and then because the name isn't that well-known. I was told that I was named after a small Indian boy in one of Dad's Wisconsin parishes. I have found out, however, that *Arlo* is not an Indian name. The Native Americans, at least those in Wisconsin, don't claim it.

I've been called *Marlow, Harlow, Arno, Arnold, Carlos,* and a few other less-flattering things. One guy even thought I said, "Carload." I think he needed a new hearing aid.

The name *Arlo,* however, was better than what sister Marty told me was the alterative: *Ohnotagain.* That's what she said Dad probably said to Mom, with a sigh, when she whispered something in his ear about her condition, perhaps in January of 1928.

I really thought Dad might rather have said to Mom, with a sigh, "Finally seven." But that, as a name, would have given me much more trouble, I'm sure, than *Ohnotagain.* I'm glad they chose neither.

It's been said that *seven* is the number of completeness, but apparently our parents didn't think so; they had three more after they had me—Immanuel, Waldemar, and Daniel. Our brother Waldemar returned to be with the Lord as an infant; his grave is in Odessa. Nine grew up of the ten born to our parents.

There was a *lot of living* done in that parsonage. We were a *singing* family of devout Christians, and all of us, it seems, were endowed with the ability to sing and given *a sense of humor.*

I decided to call this book *Parsonage in a Pear Tree* because that's often the way we jokingly sang "*partridge* in a pear tree" in the "Twelve Days of Christmas." We did that just for fun.

Our father also had a sense of humor, but did not like us to joke about the Holy Scripture or sacred hymns. However, I guess the "Twelve Days of Christmas" was not considered to be sacred; I never heard any objection to our singing *"parsonage in a pear tree,"* in place of *partridge.*

There is no relationship between *partridge* and *parsonage*; the two words just sound a little alike, so we parsonage dwellers had our fun with it.

We also joked about our situation in life. We, in a country preacher's family, were not affluent, to say the least, but we said we weren't *as poor as* church mice; *we were* church mice!

I never heard anyone in the family complain, though, about having so little. We thought a plaque somebody gave Dad said it right:

SERVING THE LORD DOESN'T PAY MUCH, BUT THE RETIREMENT IS OUT OF THIS WORLD!

Our sense of humor could easily turn tears to smiles. For example, when brother Vernon was about fourteen, one day, he put his wet boots in the oven of the kitchen woodstove to dry.

Soon afterward, someone fired up the stove and accidentally shut the oven door. The result? *Baked boots*!

The boots, of course, were ruined. For Vernon, that was a tragedy. However, while he whimpered over his loss, one of the girls put the *well-done* boots on a platter, as though they were to be served for dinner. (After all, *they were baked*!) Weeping turned to laughter as we tried to help Vernon figure out where he might get another pair of used boots.

I say "used boots" because we were very much reared on *hand-me-downs* from members of the family and from *the giving hands of loving friends in the congregation.* Many of those German Lutheran families were large, and some had children near the ages of those in our family. That was fortunate for us.

The idea of hand-me-downs reminds me of another source of smiles: one of our sisters earned enough (about six dollars) to buy a new coat one winter. When she chose a red one, the sister two years younger *cried; she didn't like to wear red.*

There is one more incident where there were some serious tears. I say it was more serious because it involved money, which was as scarce as hens' teeth at our house: one time, at Christmastime, Mom was given *a card of thanks with a five-dollar bill* for her faithfulness in playing the organ for church worship services. (She received no salary for her work; this was a gift.)

As Mom and one of my sisters were chatting in the kitchen near the woodstove, Mom absentmindedly crumbled up the five-dollar bill and tossed it in the stove instead of the gum wrapper she had in her other hand.

When they realized what Mom had accidentally done, *there was weeping,* to be sure! (Five dollars could buy a lot of groceries or a pair of shoes and a housedress at that time.)

Since there was no way to rectify the situation and because I had learned that it was no use to cry over spilled milk, I (ten years old) stepped up to the stove and started to deliver a eulogy for *"Bill, who had just been cremated."* It was still hard to stop the tears, but eventually there were some smiles, and life went on.

I've written over forty episodes about my growing-up years in Odessa, which are in this book. They're not all flattering; after all, they're factual—at least as factual as my memory and lifelong notes can make them.

We Janssen siblings weren't hellions, but we weren't cherubim either. I've heard it said that the church is *a hospital for sinners,* not *a museum for saints.* I guess that's about the way it also was in our *home next door to the church.*

We sang a second stanza to the children's song "Jesus Loves Me," which I think our mother composed. It went like this:

> Jesus loves me when I'm good,
> When I do the things I should;
> Jesus loves me when I'm bad,
> Though it makes Him very sad.
> Yes, Jesus loves me; the Bible tells me so.

Various things are said about PKs (preacher's kids) in these episodes, especially, of course, about our family and very especially about the bottom side of the family, where I, as number 7, was *the oldest of the youngest.*

Manny, Danny, and I were known for years in the family as *"the three little boys."* According to German tradition, I was told by our father many, many times, "Remember that you are the oldest. Take care of your brothers." He meant, of course, the two younger than I, Manny and Danny.

It is my hope that you will enjoy reading these episodes; I certainly enjoyed writing them. They evolved from voluminous notes I kept from my early grade-school years and from vivid memories. Also, as many of our friends and relatives know, many of these *stories* have been told and retold many times *by yours truly.*

CHAPTER TWO

WHERE THERE'S SMOKE, THERE'S FIRE IN DAD'S EYES!

We learn from our mistakes.

One summer morning, when I was going on eleven and brother Manny nine, we found a cigarette package on the steps of the town hall near the Trinity Lutheran parsonage where we lived.

The pack wasn't crumpled, so we looked and found one cigarette left in it. We looked at each other, and both thought the same thing: *It would be a shame to let a perfectly good cigarette like that go to waste.* The fresh tobacco in the cigarette even smelled good. So we decided to get a match and see what smoking was like.

We chose our brother Ihno's workshop in the shed behind our house for our experiment. After a couple of puffs, sure enough, five-year-old brother Danny came into the workshop, looking for us. We offered Danny a couple of puffs, hoping that would shut him up about what we were doing. However, things never quite worked the way we wanted them with little Danny.

As soon as he puffed and coughed a little, Danny headed to the house and into Dad's study. Sister Marcia told us what happened next. Danny blew his breath into Dad's face and said, "Smell my breath, Dad. Arlo and Manny aren't smoking out in the shed. Honest, they're not."

Of course, Dad believed what Danny said like he would have if he'd said there were two elephants playing hopscotch on the sidewalk between the house and the well.

In a minute, our father was in the doorway of the workshop. The room was full of smoke. I had the cigarette in my hand, and Manny was blowing out smoke from the last drag he'd taken. What were we to do? We were caught. There's no other way to put it; we were caught! I think we felt like a crook must feel when a policeman's flashlight shines in his face.

I thought Dad's eyes were going to pop out of his head as he began a special *sermon* for us, totally without notes or manuscript, with his voice almost at full throttle!

Dad's *sermon full of fire*, of course, was delivered in German, in his native tongue. He usually spoke only German when he was angry, which, at Manny and me, was all too frequently. We weren't bad kids; we just got into monkey business at times.

Besides a barrage of words about smoking and the danger of fire, Dad marched us into his study. There was, of course, no trial, only *a sentencing*. Manny and I were assigned to an hour *at attention* in straight-back chairs in Dad's study.

Danny, Dad's *Schatze* (sweetheart), was ordered by Mom to stay out of the study during that hour. I think Danny thought he should have gotten a Medal of Honor or at least a cookie for informing on the family *brothers-turned-criminals.*

However, later he told us that he did not mean to tell on us. Of course, according to what Marty told us, we couldn't figure out what else he was doing when he blew his breath into Dad's face. Oh well, he was just a little kid; maybe he didn't realize what he was doing. Danny, it seems, could do both right and wrong at the same time and not realize which was which.

Dad wasn't a violent person, but it was bad to *ruffle his feathers,* and it was doubly bad *to get his ire up* on a Friday, his sermon-preparation day.

What was worse—he was preparing that day to preach on Sunday *in English!* Preaching in English was always harder for Dad because he wrote first in German, then translated into English. While we sat there, if we so much as cleared our throats, he would say, "Sei mal ruhig!" (Be quiet!)

After Dad calmed down a little and got back into his sermonizing, he asked me a couple of times, in a much different tone of voice, how to express an idea in English. I guess Dad knew that my English was pretty good, even if my behavior didn't always measure up to his expectations.

I didn't get time off for *good behavior,* or anything like that, for my language help. However, I knew I'd feel proud if he used in his sermon something I had suggested.

I couldn't tell anyone, though, no matter how much I may have wanted to.

The slogan for Chesterfield at that time was "They satisfy." But I can assure you that the one we lit up that day didn't do it for us. Not only did we get into trouble, but Manny and I *turned green* as we sat *straight as boards* in grim silence in those straight-back chairs.

We both wanted to head for the far reaches of the garden where we could have *a private barf session* and bury the evidence.

Finally, we were *paroled* and warned not to do that again. It was noon, our dinnertime, but I don't think Manny and I ate much. We just didn't feel like it after our experience with that Chesterfield. Because of the problem Manny and I had caused, I don't think anyone at the table spoke much that day.

The rather odd benefit of frequently getting such a barrage of *Deutsch* was that Manny and I learned a little more of the language than the others on the younger side of the family.

Of course, our experiment taught us something about smoking too, which helped us in later life.

Dad said frequently, "Von unsere Fehlern, wir lehrnen." (We learn from our mistakes.) I can assure you that brother Manny and I extended our education in several ways that day when we found that cigarette on the town hall steps.

We realized too late that we should have left it for the pack rats that sometimes wandered over that way from the old jail behind the town hall.

CHAPTER THREE

DUCKS IN THE PARSONAGE YARD?

"Chicks and ducks and geese better scurry," they sang in the musical *Oklahoma*. We never had any geese in the parsonage yard in Odessa, but we did have chickens at times, and there were two summers when Manny and I raised some ducks.

I got the idea from Roger Pansch when I stayed with him for a week or so on his folks' farm between Odessa and Correll. Roger and I were about ten, which would make it about 1938.

Roger was full of ideas, but not all his ideas were good. Like, one day Roger suggested that we "rope" a calf like they do in a rodeo. We got the rope on the calf's neck, in the barnyard, and I gave a powerful pull while the calf was trying to get away. Down the poor calf went. There it lay, not moving a muscle.

We panicked because we thought the calf was dead. I prayed that the Lord would raise the calf again to life! Roger had a different idea; he loosened the rope and gave her a little kick with his bare foot. All of a sudden the calf got up and ran away.

We argued a little bit about which did the most good—my prayer or his actions. He argued that the calf was just out of breath because of my sudden pull when she was trying to run away. Maybe he was right, but we were sure happy that the calf was okay, and we didn't have to tell Roger's dad, Henry, what had happened.

I liked Henry Pansch, but he was kind of a no-nonsense guy. I don't think he'd have been too happy about having to butcher a calf on a Saturday afternoon because we had accidentally killed it.

The idea about raising ducks, on the other hand, was really interesting to me; I wanted to know more. Roger was happy to explain what to do and how to do it. He even told about caring for chicken cluck that has to sit on the eggs for twenty-one days. Also, he explained why and how we'd have to candle the eggs every day after the first week to check if something was developing inside. I was sure Manny and I could do it, if our parents would agree.

At first Mom and Dad weren't too enthusiastic about it. They relented, however, when we promised that we would do all the work. Also, they thought a little differently about it when we said this was not going to be a business venture, but a way to help the family.

The next spring, Manny and I earned enough money to buy ten duck eggs, and we borrowed a clucking chicken hen from the Hammonds, who were living in the Immanuel parsonage in Yellow Bank at that time.

After the first week, we candled the eggs every day at a knothole on the side of the barn to see if there were tiny ducklings forming in the eggs. Also, we diligently took care of the cluck; she had to be taken off the nest twice a day so she could eat, drink, and take care of *her other basic needs*.

Would you believe, all the ten eggs hatched! It was fascinating to see those eggs become ducklings! Real, live ducks!

After they grew some, it was fun to watch the chicken hen try to be a good mother to her brood of ducks. She did a pretty good job with the ducklings, but when *her little ones* went for a swim in the tub of water we "buried" in the yard for them, the chicken hen almost *lost her mind!*

I guess she thought her little *chicks* were going to say good-bye to the world and sink to the bottom of the tubs of water. She didn't realize that they were not her dryland-lover flesh and blood, but water-loving, web-footed ducks.

At first, to feed the ducks and their surrogate mother, we got some grain by helping a farmer on the outskirts of Odessa pull mustard weeds out of his grain field.

Later in the summer, that same farmer let us pick up as much grain as we could from what was spilled around the threshing machine and around the door of his granary. Also, he gave us nearly a bushel of oats for helping clean up around the threshing rig for several days.

The next spring, we bought two dozens duck eggs and borrowed three clucking chicken hens. Manny and I diligently took care of those three hens and candled the eggs regularly for the three weeks that the hens sat on the nests to hatch the eggs.

We couldn't believe it, but twenty-three of the twenty-four eggs produced beautiful little ducklings. Having that many and three hens made for more work, but Manny and I managed it again, helping that same farmer pull mustard weeds and generally helping him, especially at threshing time.

He was very good to us because he knew we were raising the ducks to help the family. Near the end of summer, however, we needed to buy a bushel of corn for the ducks. By that time, they were no longer little ducklings. They were almost full-grown and gobbling the food down like little pigs! They ate a lot!

We went house to house asking people if they wanted their lawns mowed. We found two who said yes that day. The people offered a quarter to have their lawns mowed, which took us a couple of hours each. Also, we were lucky enough to get a dime tip at one of the homes because the *lady* paid us, not the man. Her husband, a local blacksmith, wasn't always that kind to us, and he thought laborers, especially kids, were overpaid.

The blacksmith's wife said Manny and I were "such cute twins." Actually, we weren't twins; we looked somewhat alike, I guess, because we both wore the same cutoff bib overalls and had similar short crew cuts "styled" by Mrs. August Anderson. Also, we were both barefoot.

We didn't tell the lady, though; we let her think we were twins. She was pretty deaf anyway; it was hard for her to understand us.

That dime tip brought us up to the sixty cents. That's what we were told a bushel of corn would cost. We went to a grain elevator in downtown Odessa, having our money in hand and pulling a coaster wagon with an empty gunnysack in it.

However, when Mr. Bohn, the elevator manager, helped us put the corn in our sack, and we got it on our wagon, he said the cost was *seventy-five cents.*

Manny and I looked at each other. Then I shyly told Mr. Bohn that we had only sixty cents, which was what we were told it would cost. Manny also said with his head down, "We earned the sixty cents mowing two really big lawns!" And I added, "And we got an extra dime from one lady who likes us."

Mr. Bohn thought for a moment, then sat down at his desk, and surely acted like he was reading from his book. Then he looked at us seriously and asked, "Are you boys raising these ducks to sell?"

"No, sir," I replied very seriously, "we're just trying to help our family have something special for winter Sunday dinners or Thanksgiving." And Manny almost whispered, "Maybe even for Christmas."

Mr. Bohn swung back around on his swivel desk chair and again seemed to be reading in his book. Finally, he said, "It says here that for duck raisers who are doing it for their family and not to make money, the cost for a bushel of corn is just sixty cents today." Then he added, looking down at his book once more, "That is, if they're willing to sweep the elevator office and the truck scale."

We almost cheered! Needless to say, the big push brooms he gave us to use made the dust fly for the next hour in his office and on the truck scale!

That afternoon we were two happy boys when one of us pulled and the other pushed that wagon home with our sack of corn. And the ducks enjoyed a special dinner that night.

A FOLLOW-UP STORY

When I read to a friend the above story about raising ducks, he told me this story. I hope you enjoy it as much as I did.

A duck one day entered a grocery store and asked an employee, "Got any duck food?"

"No," was the abrupt answer. "Now, get out of here!"

The next day the duck entered the same store and asked the same employee, "Got any duck food?"

"No!" the man shouted. "We don't have duck food! And if you come in here again, I'll nail your webbed feet to the floor!"

The next day the duck again came in and asked the employee, "Got any nails?"

"No!" the man answered angrily. "Why are you asking such a dumb question?"

"Got any duck food?" asked the duck, with a smile on his bill.

CHAPTER FOUR

CHRISTMAS AT THE PARSONAGE

And it came to pass in those days . . .
—Luke 2:1

Christmas was always a wonderful time at the parsonage. There weren't a lot of gifts like many children have today, but we had each other in our large family, and *we joyfully celebrated the Savior's coming to the world to be our Savior! It was a spiritual time, and it was always enjoyable!*

We had a Christmas tree every year, which usually came from the Yellow Bank woods. We sometimes decorated it with all blue lights, which gave a warm feeling. And along with tinsel and homemade decorations, we had some little glass ornaments from Germany. Those were special because they were gifts from Dad's loved ones.

Mom and the girls crisscrossed red-and-green crepe paper ribbon in our front room, from the center ceiling light to the corners of the front room. Even the potbellied stove seemed more festive at Christmas, although to some of the family, the pipe to the ceiling wasn't so pretty.

People in Odessa didn't have to decorate *outside* their houses. *God did it*, usually right in time for Christmas Eve, with a *mantel of white*—on trees, bushes, fence posts, housetops, and even on backyard pumps. Cardinals, blue jays, and winter-fluffy chickadees in the trees also seemed to add to the decorations.

Most people in the village put their Christmas tree in a front window, which helped to dress up the town. The Kollitzes always decorated in their store window too and put some toys on display about the middle of December. All this added to the warmth of the holy season and reminded us that the greatest gift was the Savior, Jesus.

When I walked home after delivering my papers around Christmastime, it looked like the whole village was ready for the celebration of the Lord's coming into the world.

Bethlehem in Judea couldn't have looked any prettier, except maybe in the stable on the first Christmas, with the shepherds gathered around and even the animals seeming to adore the baby Jesus.

The Saturdays before Christmas, we had practice for the Christmas program at church. Melinda Pansch directed the program at Trinity in Odessa. She was a good teacher, but it bothered me sometimes that she noticed everything.

To give an example, she asked me once during our practice why I had a look on my face like the cat that ate the canary. (That look so often betrayed me in my childhood.)

I didn't dare tell Mrs. Pansch how Plink Gutzman and Junior Mews in the back row were recomposing or adding lines to a few of the songs she was teaching us to sing.

For instance, when we sang the Latin "In Dulce Jubilo," they added the rhyme *"it's twenty-two below"*; and the German *"Mach hoch die Tur, die Tor mach veit,"* was followed with *"venn ve get done, ve go outside."*

Dear Melinda's hairpins would have flipped out and stuck to the high ceiling of the church if I'd told her that Glen and Erich's "amended carols" were tickling my funny bone; hence, the look on my face.

At Immanuel in Yellow Bank, the program was mostly in German in the thirties and was directed by our mother, assisted by Cora Fitzner.

When I participated in the Yellow Bank Christmas program the first time at about age four, they told me that I said I was told by my mother to speak so I could be heard *"all the way to the cemetery"* (about fifty yards from the church). I guess that wasn't actually what she had told me to say, but at that age, that was my version.

In the Yellow Bank church, there was no electricity in the '30s, so they had *real candles on the Christmas tree.* I can still see Albert Ell and Willy Mueller stand guard with wet cloths during the Christmas service. Dangerous as it may have been, it was beautiful with candles on the tree and decorated lamps hanging from the high ceiling in the church.

It was nice to have snow at Christmas, but it wasn't so pretty if it snowed and the wind blew when we had to drive home from Yellow Bank on a dark Christmas night.

I think it was in about 1933 that it snowed so furiously when we were on our way home from Yellow Bank that *Dad opened the windshield a little on our '26 Essex, and Vernon, about nine, worked the hand-operated windshield wiper to help Dad see.*

Sister Marcia sat beside Vernon in the front seat and coached him. (The four oldest—Ihno, Ruth, Anita, and Adie—were not with us. I think they were caroling for shut-ins with the Youth Group in Odessa.)

Manny and I were snuggled with Mom in the backseat that cold snowy night in the fur robe made for us by Grandpa Reddepennig. Daniel, J., number 10, the last one in the family, had not as yet been born. In fact, in December of 1933, Danny wasn't even on the way yet; he was born in November of 1934.

We all prayed a lot as Dad, who wasn't the world's best driver, drove *lansam und vorsichtig* (slowly and carefully) the four miles of windblown gravel road to Odessa. With God's help, we made it home that night *"over the tip of Antarctica"* (we kids said), that is, across the Minnesota River and into our little town, Odessa.

Speaking of snow, I remember the Christmas of 1938, when the storm was so severe that *we had no church services on Christmas Eve or Christmas Day in Odessa or Yellow Bank.* (Even the second Christmas Day, German service had to be cancelled.) There were a lot of snowstorms in those years in Minnesota. However, in my memory, *the blizzard of 1938 was the only one right at Christmas.*

On Christmas night, people were thankful to make it to the woodshed for fuel in that storm. *No one could go anywhere else,* so the supposed children's program on Christmas Eve and the Christmas-morning service were postponed.

That Christmas night, we had our own program in the parsonage. As the wind whistled outside, we each recited our program parts to the family, and we sang all the Christmas carols in the program and many more. Mom and sister Ruth played the piano, and Dad and some of us read the scriptures.

Then we opened gifts. There wasn't much said about Santa Claus at our house. As children, we knew "the man in red-and-white" was from a book, and we knew that book wasn't the Prophecy of Isaiah or the Gospel of Luke. And we joked saying that even if Santa could find little Odessa, it would be a bit difficult for him to get in our house through the potbellied stove.

I'm sure our realizing that *gifts had to be bought or homemade* made us more satisfied with and thankful for *new mittens, long johns, or flannel shirts.* Also, we always looked forward to the Christmas bags at church, with candy, nuts, and even an apple and an orange. We loved the gifts too of food and used clothing and shoes from the parishioners.

Another special gift: the Kollitzes gave us *a whole box of apples* every Christmas. And best of all, the entire family was together that snowstorm Christmas! What more would a child want? And above all, *we had the gift of God's love given to us in Jesus the Savior!*

Before we went to bed during that Christmas Eve blizzard, we all gathered around the big kitchen table for a wonderful lunch. After we had special Christmas prayers, Dad and Mother announced that the homemade bread was made by Mrs. Augie Gutzman, the smoked sausage by the Max Schmeichel family, sauerkraut by Grandpa and Grandma Pomerenke, and the berry sauce was from Aunt Mary and Uncle Stromer in Wisconsin. *All those gifts added to the joy!*

Christmas morning in 1938, the storm was still raging, so after we got wood and coal in the house from the shed and stoked up the stoves, we had our own Christmas service, with everyone in the family participating, even four-year-old Danny.

After Dad stood by the Christmas tree and informally delivered a sermon in both English and German, he asked us, "What did I preach about?" Danny answered, *"About an hour."* Dad didn't appreciate that answer too much, but he did manage to laugh with the rest of us. Danny was, after all, Dad's *Kleine Schatze* (little darling); Dad never got too mad about anything Danny did or said.

For dinner in the middle of that storm we had roast ducks, a gift from the Emil Steffen family, and cranberries from Wisconsin. We had a blessed and very enjoyable Christmas Day, even though the wind blew so hard that *the square-box parsonage* creaked like it was going to take off from its foundation and blow into South Dakota.

It was a special gift that Ihno and Ruth, the oldest brother and sister, were with us that Christmas! In the afternoon of Christmas Day, Ruth played Christmas carols on the piano, and all of us sang. We all loved to sing, and we were all pretty good at it. *You should have heard the pickup harmony when we all sang together!*

Then, Ihno organized all kinds of games. He even made up an exciting tournament of putting together the simple fifty-piece puzzles we'd received as gifts at school. Then we had fudged popcorn, a special recipe of Mom's.

Would you believe—in the middle of the afternoon, with the snow still blowing so you almost couldn't see your hand in front of your face, *there was a knock on our front door!* We couldn't imagine who would be at the door in the middle of such a raging storm! It was Uncle Walter Thormaehlen, Mother's brother!

Walter was almost like a brother to us. He was about the same age as our sister Ruth and had been brought up partly with our family. (His mother, Grandma Thormaehlen, had died when he was born *in the Yellow Bank parsonage*, in 1917.)

Walter, who joined the army the next summer and served in North Africa during much of World War II, was still a college student in 1938. He had made it to Uncle Erich and Aunt Clara Mews's house the day of Christmas Eve before the worst of the snowstorm hit. Phones were out because of the storm, so we didn't know he was just across town (about four blocks) from our house!

He had almost crawled the several blocks through the storm to our house! It was great to see him. His coming to our house added to the joy of Christmas! With a family the size of ours, there was always room for one more—especially Uncle Walter!

Even though the festival services and programs were postponed that year till close to New Year's because of the snowstorm, it was surely a wonderful, though snowy, cold Christmas at the Trinity parsonage!

Oh yes, several times that Christmas we again sang the "Twelve Days of Christmas" with our special words: "*and a* parsonage *in a pear tree.*"

CHAPTER FIVE

BATH IN A SNOWSTORM?

Cleanliness is next to godliness.

Why would you suppose all the boys in the house would get *a bath during a snowstorm*? And it wasn't even Saturday! As you might know, there's a story behind this.

First, let me tell you something about snowstorms in that part of the country. The terrain is fairly flat around the village of Odessa, in western Minnesota, near the South Dakota border. We always said you could almost see down the railroad tracks from Odessa to the grain elevators in Correll, nine miles to the east. Well, it wasn't quite that flat, but almost.

On such a flat plain, when a couple inches of snow would fall on a very cold day, you had to watch out—*even when it was so calm—that snow would accumulate on the tiniest tree branch! With the sudden start-up of wind, a snowstorm could come to visit, even* when it wasn't expected or invited, and certainly not welcomed.

Very cold snow can be as fine as dust. If a wind comes up, you can have a *whiteout* in minutes. Visibility, almost zero! That happened frequently in that part of Minnesota.

The snowstorm I'm thinking about right now was, I'm pretty sure, in February of 1939. Fine, almost-powdery snow started falling around noon and continued on and on and just didn't quit.

The white blanket was beautiful at first as the fine snow sifted down. All was still as snow piled up on the tree branches and the tiniest of limbs and twigs, tops of fence posts, and even on thin fence wire. It was a virtual *winter wonderland!*

Suddenly a wind arose and got stronger by the minute, sometimes coming in gusts that could knock a person down! Soon it was difficult to see your hand in front of your face! In no time, it seemed, it was *a blinding snowstorm!*

I've lived in places, like Philadelphia, Pennsylvania, where they called it a *snowstorm* when a little snow fell. In western Minnesota, they would say when snow started to fall, *"It's snowing."* And life would go on as usual.

However, fine snow falling, being blown by gusts of wind, believe me, was a storm! *You couldn't call it anything else, and you had to look out* when such a storm hit!

The February snowfall in 1939 *indeed became a* snowstorm in almost no time at all, and it got worse by the minute. The school administrators got the busses to the school, but it was too late. By the time they arrived, the drivers couldn't see past the hood ornaments through the windshield of the bus!

Darkness came early in the middle of winter. Less light meant more danger for the busses driving in the country. This truly turned into a blizzard—too late for the busses to take the rural children home. Before school was to be dismissed, it was decided to arrange for the rural students to stay in town for the night.

If there were 180 students in the twelve grades in the Odessa school, probably a hundred thirty of them were from rural areas, transported by busses. Some of the children rode the bus an hour in the afternoon even in good weather. Who knows how long it would take if the driver couldn't always see the road! In fact, they could end up *in the middle of nowhere*, where they couldn't move at all!

When all the rural students had to stay in town, every home in the village with students in the school would have to take several rural pupils home for the night.

Although we had six children in our family still at home, our parents took five of the country kids that day.

When we had as many as we always did in our house, it seems there was always room for one more. Anyway, *the parsonage was always a kind of sanctuary for those in need*. It was, at least, when our family lived in the Trinity parsonage.

Along with the kids assigned to us, I brought home a boy in my class who was different. I'll call him "Ned."

Some boys ridiculed Ned—the way he dressed and the hillbilly way he talked. Also, he was not the cleanest.

Ned's mother had died when he was small; he was reared by his dad, kind of a mountain man farmhand. The two of them lived in a cabin on a farm in the woods north of Odessa. I couldn't let Ned go to a place where people wouldn't understand him, so I asked to take him with me.

In the storm that afternoon, we had a hard-enough time walking to our house, but we made it, taking a half-dozen extra kids along with us, including Ned. Our parents welcomed all of them and assured them that they were a part of our family during their stay with us.

While our Mom was preparing dinner for *the snowstorm group* and Dad and my sisters were preparing places for everyone to sleep (some with blankets on the floor), sister Marty and I had the job of helping the "guests" wash up.

As I was helping Ned wash, I noticed that there was caked dirt on his wrists and on his neck. When I whispered to Mom what I had found, she immediately said to Dad, in German, "We'll have to bathe that boy."

When Dad heard that, he immediately told Mom (also in German), "Don't give *just one boy* a bath. That will humiliate him!" So what was Mom's decision? To give *all boys in the house* a bath!

Giving baths was not a minor operation since all water had to be pumped up from the cistern (under the kitchen) and heated on the kitchen stove in a large copper boiler. Nonetheless, *all of us boys were bathed that night*, one by one, in a galvanized tub in the washroom.

Sometimes we used the same water for more than one boy, but Dad changed the water after Ned had his bath. We didn't tell him why, though. We just said it was time to change the water, so Ned didn't think anything of it.

Then we all needed clean clothes. Fortunately, brother Manny's *long johns* (winter underwear) fit Ned. His underwear was almost falling apart; he'd probably worn them continuously since fall. I wouldn't doubt it if he'd even slept in it.

After dinner, our dad led us all in a devotion. While we listened to Dad read scripture to us and offer words of comfort, we could hear the wind whistle around the big old square parsonage like it was trying to blow it out of western Minnesota into Dakota, or even entirely off the face of the earth!

As we bedded down, Dad stopped at each bed and by those of us whose "bed" was blankets on the floor and assured us all that we were in God's hands. Also, he had prayer with all of us at each bed.

The boys were the cleanest kids in the house that night, especially for a day that *wasn't even Saturday!* I think Ned felt especially good, although I'm sure he didn't know that he was the cause of the *snowstorm bath night.*

Those of us who had to sleep on the floor next to our friend Ned that night were happy too. All of us boys were clean as a whistle, smelling more like Ivory soap than like weeks- or months-old sweat, no matter how hard earned it may have been.

CHAPTER SIX

SLIDING ON THE HILLS IN ODESSA

Over the hills and through the woods
was always fun.

When I had to climb the hill in Odessa to attend school, I sometimes wondered why the school was built up there. Climbing that hill was a special drudge when I knew that a long division test was scheduled for the first hour of the morning. With every step, I tried to reason what long division had to do with life.

There were times, however, when the school hill was where many of the village kids gathered—to have fun with sleds and other instruments used for *one of the great winter pastimes we called* sliding. *We had a lot of fun on that hill, in various places, when there was a mantel of white covering the ground in the winter.*

We spent hours on the hill with our sleds and other devices used to ride down when the snow was just right. Sometimes there must have been fifteen or more village kids having a good time together after school and on the weekends.

There were several places on the *"school hill"* in Odessa where we went *sliding*. I know in many parts of the country it's called *sledding*, and maybe that sounds more correct, but we in Odessa called it *sliding*.

No matter what it's called, we had a lot of fun on the hill on regular *sleds, bobsleds*, and sometimes *scoop shovels* and even *dishpans*. By regular sleds, I mean the store-bought kind with narrow metal runner ones you could steer because the runners bent a little with a steering device in front.

Some sleds were short, the kind you could run and fall on to get a head start. Brother Danny won a small sled like that one time by writing a letter to Santa. He was only about six at the time. I think he was encouraged to write the letter by sister Marcia. Maybe she helped him a little too.

Some sleds were longer, with room enough for two or three kids, depending on the kid's size. I have an exact replica of one of those hanging on the wall in my study here in our home in Southern Arizona. It reminds me of the fun we had sliding on the hills in Odessa when I was a boy.

On the longer sleds, the kid riding on the back would give a mighty running push, then jump onto the sled behind the others. We did it something like they do in the bobsled competition in the Winter Olympics. Fortunately, of course, we didn't travel downhill as fast as they do.

The bobsleds we had were nothing like those called bobsleds in the Olympics. *Ours were fashioned after the big bobsleds pulled by horses at that time.*

We in our family had a bobsled that our father had made, which was a perfect replica of the horse-drawn type. It was made in three parts—the front, with runners; the back part, with another set of runners; and the flat-board platform that fit over the front and back when they were hooked together. The runners on our bobsled were made of wood, with a metal strip fastened to the edge to make them more slippery. It's hard to explain, but *it was quite a sled.* Our father, who had been a ship's carpenter in Germany before he came to America, designed and built it; it was beautiful. We called it Dad's *Meisterstueck* (masterpiece).

Our bobsled also had a handle on it, which made it just right for pulling to give a child a ride. I rather think that the sled was made for Mother or Dad to pull one or two of the children when they were small. Dad made it when the family lived in Milan, Wisconsin, where there were no hills like we had in Odessa.

We also used scoop shovels at times, especially when we slid down the steep banks of the gravel pits—the pit in the DeWaldses' pasture or the pit between the two roads up the hill to the school.

Running and jumping onto a shovel was fun, but I guess it was a little dangerous. I don't remember that anyone was seriously hurt, though, but I do recall that a few kids went home crying at times. There were times too when we even used old dishpans to do some of the same things in the gravel pits and on other steep inclines.

We weren't supposed to use the school hill road for sliding on school days until all the traffic was gone after school. If no one was looking, though, some of us in our family took a ride on a sled to get down near our house at lunchtime. We could make it as far as Schuett's, then cut through their yard to our house.

I don't know what anyone would have done if they had caught us sliding on the road in the middle of the day. The town marshal was almost never around.

There were times when that school hill road was the best place to go sliding, though, and we really had fun there after school—sometimes till dark—and on Saturdays and Sunday afternoons.

When the packed snow was just right and more than one was on the sled to give it some weight, we could sometimes make it almost all the way down to the old town hall, or at least to the *church square,* the block before that.

Sometimes on the school hill, we'd try "bulldogging," which meant we'd try to jump from one sled to another when we were going the fastest down the hill. (I suppose the term "bulldogging" came from the rodeo.)

Bulldogging was a little dangerous too. In fact, it was more dangerous for the sleds than it was for us kids. More than once, I remember taking our *Flexible Flyer* to Augie Anderson's blacksmith shop to get the runners fixed.

The other side of the school hill was fun to slide on too. I mean the school hill road that went past Stegners.

We didn't use that hill quite as much, though. Probably we didn't use that hill as much because it was steeper. Also, because of the steeper incline, it wasn't used much by vehicles in the winter, so the snow wasn't packed down, just right for sliding, like it was on the other road.

Another place we had a lot of fun sliding was down the hill through the DeWaldses' pasture to the road between Draffehns and Von Eschens (where Albert Schwants lived earlier). Sliding down that hill, we'd sometimes make it all the way to the parsonage and Holman's house across the street.

Kids from our family and Holman's used that hill the most often. The Holmans had a family almost as large as ours, and a number of them were pretty much the same age as we were. Also, the Virgil Gloege family—three girls, if I recall correctly—were frequently with us. Kids from other parts of town often joined us there too.

That hill was really fun, but to cut down the danger, we snipped the pasture fence wires. I guess the DeWaldses didn't mind too much, though. I never heard that they complained. There were, of course, no cows in the pasture at that time of the year.

The only problem was that they had to mend the fence before they did use it for cows in the spring. But I don't recall that the DeWaldses ever made a fuss about the extra work. Maybe they thought, "Let the kids have their fun!"

There was a bump about halfway to the fence line on that hill, which added to the thrill of the ride. If the snow was packed just right, with a small sled, we'd almost take off when we went over that bump! It was a lot of fun!

There were times when I wondered why they built the Odessa school on that hill; I even wondered why the village of Odessa was built where it was.

I know this, though, that it was great having that hill where it was. We had a lot of fun on that hill with sleds in Odessa when we were children in the thirties and early forties.

I wonder if kids still use the hills. If they don't, they're missing something, in my opinion.

CHAPTER SEVEN

ICE SKATING IN AND NEAR ODESSA

Over the river and through the town . . .

Much of our ice skating in the Odessa area was done on the Minnesota River, about a mile from town. There were times, however, when there were places to skate right in the town. That's *skating* I'm talking about, not ice fishing.

That reminds me of an ice-fishing story someone told me here in Arizona. The fellow who told me this story was originally from Sioux Falls, South Dakota.

This man said that an old man (he had to be old) was drilling a hole in the ice one day with the intention of going fishing. All of a sudden he heard someone call out, "There is no fishing allowed here!" The old guy couldn't figure out what was happening, so he went on with his drilling.

Again, the voice was heard; this time it thundered, "No fishing here!" The man still continued his drilling.

Then the voice really boomed out, *"This is the manager of this rink!* There is no fishing here! Please put on your skates, or leave the area!"

At the end of this chapter about our *skating in Odessa* in the thirties and early forties, I'll relate to you another story about ice fishing.

We did a lot of ice skating in and around Odessa when I was a child. I wonder whether kids there today get away from TV and video games to have fun like we did. They should; we surely enjoyed many hours on the ice.

The best place to skate usually was on the Minnesota River. I wrote something about that in the chapter of this book about *what it was like to come home* from skating *on December 7, 1941, to find out that the U.S. base at Pearl Harbor had been bombed.* What a jolt it was to go from the happiness of skating with friends to finding out that our country was being drawn into a World War!

We did have fun that December day, until we got home. The river was just about perfect for skating that day. It wasn't always that way.

The river was usually a very good place to skate. I say "usually" because there were times when the river froze the hardest *while it was snowing.* If there was snow mixed into the ice on the surface of the river, it was not very good for skating. If the water on the river didn't "open up" again (thaw and refreeze), it could be that way for the whole winter. Consequently, skating would have to be done somewhere else when that happened.

The best was *when the river froze when it was calm* and not snowing. Sometimes, the ice was perfect for the whole winter because the conditions were just right when it froze hard in late fall. Even if snow fell on the river later, after it froze hard, it was usually still good for skating.

Snow could always be shoveled to clear an area much *like a skating rink*. We just had to stay pretty much in the area we had shoveled clear.

When we had to clear an area for skating, we just couldn't very easily skate "down the river" like we did December 7, 1941. (I told about that in that chapter.) That wasn't a big problem, though; we could clear enough ice to make it like *a beautiful rink* most of the time.

Unless the snow was very deep on the frozen river, we made the "rink" we cleared big enough for different activities—figure skating practice and "competition," different kinds of tag, and even playing "crack the whip."

One thing we had to be careful on the river was to avoid *open places* where there was no ice because water there was moving, swirling around rocks.

The place on the river where we usually skated was not very deep; however, even to step into the water up to our knees was dangerous because the water was very cold, and there was nowhere nearby to dry off. Feet could freeze (get severely frostbitten) before a person could get back to the village if it was really cold.

We did build a warming fire most of the time, but if we didn't have an extra pair of sox, to change from the wet ones, we could still have a problem if our feet got wet.

We didn't always have to go to the river to skate. Sometimes, especially in early spring, there were ponds that formed in town. One formed quite often in George Gloege's pasture, just a few blocks from the parsonage.

Also, sometimes there was a big pond that formed across the old road, more or less behind the Reformed Church.

One year, I remember there was a very large pond there that attracted almost every kid in town who skated. I even remember that there were several teachers who came there to skate. Several of the young grade-school teachers were pretty good skaters, especially if they had grown up in one of the northern states. It was fun to have them with us kids.

Mr. Pagel, the superintendent of the Odessa school, also skated there a number of times. He was quite a skater as I recall. He too had grown up in one of the northern states where ice skating was a popular activity.

There were times too when we got our dad to skate with us. He had grown up in Northern Germany and was a very graceful skater.

I remember two different times in late spring when almost the whole town was flooded, and it froze solid. That was not good for people to get around in cars or even on foot. But it sure was fun for us kids. We could literally skate all over the village!

An icy condition like that lasted for days; I think one of those times it was a week or more. If I remember correctly, *it was after Easter*, believe it or not. Maybe that was a year when Easter was early, like it is this year (2008), when it's March 23, one day from the earliest it can be.

One of those times when the whole town was flooded, it was because the Minnesota River had gone over its banks. When that happened, quite a few fish, believe it or not, came up to see what Odessa was like. Some people who knew how to handle such situations *hooked some of those fish* into joining them at the dinner table.

That reminds me of the ice-fishing story I said I was going to tell you. I heard a ninety-year-old man tell this on a TV program on which he was being interviewed.

This elderly gentleman said that two men were fishing through a hole in the ice. Although they had all the modern equipment for ice fishing, they were catching nothing.

Quite near them, a young boy was pulling in fish, one after another. The men were wondering how this could happen; after all, they knew how to go about fishing through the ice, and they had better equipment than the kid seemed to have. So they asked the boy. The kid mumbled something the men did not understand, so they asked him again.

This time, the boy cupped his hand to his mouth and seemed to be spitting something into it. Then he said very clearly, "Ya gotta keep the worms warm."

I'm sure ice fishing is enjoyable, but I'd rather go skating on the ice, anytime, *with or without warm worms.*

CHAPTER EIGHT

GOD PROVIDES; THAT'S ALL THERE IS TO IT!

Before they call, I will answer . . .
  —Isaiah 65:24

"*God provides,*" our pastor father frequently said, "*that's all there is to it!*" It took a strong faith for our parents to truly believe that, especially with nine children—all at home—during the Depression in the early '30s.

There was no doubt, however, that *our father and mother did believe that God provided! In fact, I'm sure that they believed that so fervently that they could say,* "We *know* God provides!"

It must have been a real test with so many mouths to feed and bodies to clothe. Our parents were married in 1916. Their tenth child was born by 1934 at the height of the Depression. Nine lived and grew up of the ten. With all of us born when times were very trying for our parents, they truly must always have felt very strongly that *God provides!*

In the early '30s, there was not only a financial depression, but also a *terrible drought* in much of the midsection of the nation, including western Minnesota, where we lived. Almost nothing was growing in the fields of Dad's parishioners but Russian thistle (today called tumbleweeds).

About the only place grain grew fairly well during the drought was in the *dried-up sloughs,* which the farmers had plowed up and planted. There was no way to irrigate at that time, and there was very little water available anywhere, anyway.

Just imagine—at *that difficult time,* there were in our home, counting our parents, *eleven around the dinner table three times a day*!

Our father's salary as a country pastor was unbelievably low at that time—about seven hundred dollars a year—and that was often not paid.

When farm families in rural congregations had little income, the pastor had *very* little. What helped to an extent was that those committed Christian farmers and their wives sometimes shared with the pastor and his family the little they had.

When the farmers had grain to harvest, members of our family, including our father, helped those who wanted our assistance with their fieldwork at times. In appreciation, we were given flour for baking, made from the grain, or feed for our chickens.

When the farmers had animals to butcher, Mom and Dad as well as some of the rest of us helped with the work, and we were given sausage or some of whatever was prepared.

Also, we often received *hand-me-down* clothing and shoes from parishioners who had large families and children near the age of some of us.

Some interesting stories were told by our father about *how the Lord provides in mysterious ways*. One involved our mother's brother-in-law, Fritz Mueller. Uncle Fritz was struggling to make ends meet with his own family on a mediocre farm in the Yellow Bank area near the Dakota border. No matter how little Uncle Fritz had, he had an amazing Christian faith and compassion for our family.

Uncle Fritz one time was able to sell some hogs, for which he was paid twenty-five dollars. Being not only our uncle, but also an officer in the rural parish in Yellow Bank, which Dad served, Fritz Mueller knew that our father earned very little and was often not paid his salary.

Uncle Fritz decided to give to our parents $10 of the $25 he was paid for his hogs. (Ten dollars was, I'm sure, like $100 or more in buying power today.)

When Dad related that story in his personal life and in his confirmation classes, he was always choked up and had tears in his eyes. One reason was that, as amazing as Uncle Fritz's love for us was, *more amazing was what happened soon afterward*!

The week after Uncle Fritz shared with our family ten dollars of the twenty-five he received from selling hogs, he received in the mail the *payment of a $20 loan* he had made to a fellow soldier during the war in 1918—*more that fifteen years earlier!*

Uncle Fritz had long forgotten the loan. The soldier friend was from another part of the country, and Fritz Mueller had not seen him, nor had he heard from him in all those years.

Was that a coincidence that Uncle Fritz received that money right after he shared with our family? Our father didn't think so. He believed that Uncle Fritz was actually *repaid twofold what he gave to our family.*

We asked Dad if Uncle Fritz wouldn't have received that twenty-dollar repayment even if he had *not* helped our family. Dad calmly answered in his native tongue, "Es macht kein Unterschied." (It makes no difference.) Then he added, "God works in mysterious ways."

We also asked Dad if maybe that repayment was already decided upon by the fellow soldier and perhaps put in the mail *before* Uncle Fritz shared what he had with our family. Dad's confident answer to that was simply, "God says of His people, 'Before they call, I will answer, and while they are yet speaking, I will hear.' That's all there is to it!"

Indeed, *that's all there was to it, as far as he was concerned.* Incidentally, I found the passage of Scripture to which Dad was referring; it's *Isaiah 65:24*.

Our family made it through the Depression and drought, and God further provided for us. All the nine who grew up finished high school, and we all worked in honest professions and vocations. Also, largely by helping each other in various ways, six of the nine earned a master's degree or more at colleges and universities.

Also, all remained faithful to the Lord, and six of the nine served as professional church workers in several different capacities at one time or other; three even became ordained pastors and three others, Christian schoolteachers.

I never heard members of our large family complain about any kind of struggle they had to endure. All often repeated Dad's favorite saying: "God provides!"

The poet William Cowper said it in words that have been for over two hundred years sung as a much-loved Christian hymn:

> God moves in a mysterious way
> His wonders to perform;
> He plants His footsteps in the sea
> And rides upon the storm.
>
> Deep in unfathomable mines
> Of never failing skill
> He treasures up His bright designs
> And works His sov'reign will.
>
> Blind unbelief is sure to err
> And scan His work in vain;
> God is His own Interpreter,
> And He will make it plain.

CHAPTER NINE

FARMED OUT AS A CHILD

Home is where the heart is.

No matter how many children there were in our household, *I loved being at home, with the family.* That old square-box house—the parsonage of Trinity Lutheran Church in Odessa—was *our castle*! It was *our home*, where the family lived, ate, slept, and prayed. The main advantage of living in that parsonage, in my opinion, was that we were with our family, and it seemed that we lived *a little closer to God.*

There were, however, times when we were farmed out with other families. At a very early age, probably about seven, I stayed most of a summer on a farm with a couple that had no children.

I found out years later that the woman had had three miscarriages, so they were thinking of adopting. In fact, they were thinking of adopting a child about my age. In this way, they were more or less *testing the waters* by having me with them for a while, to see what it would be like to have a child with them.

I thought at first my stay with them was going to be only a short time, but it ended up to be about six or seven weeks, much of the summer, it seemed.

I must have gotten along with them fairly well, and I suppose they liked having me with them for some reason. They were good people, but they were not much like our mom and dad. In a way, it was enjoyable to be *the only child* for a change, but I very much missed being with our family, no matter if I was e pluribus unum (one of many) at our house.

The man and his wife with whom I stayed that summer weren't very physical in their showing love, like my parents were. The woman was more loving than her husband. He was a little stern, perhaps not understanding too well how to treat a child of my age.

His own upbringing may have been quite different from what I was used to in our home. Maybe that's what made the difference in how he treated me.

The woman, who was probably in her early thirties, seemed to understand children more than her husband did. For example, when she took me with her fishing on the banks of the Minnesota River about a half mile away from their house, she taught me things like how to put a worm on a hook, how to be patient, not too hasty in pulling in a fish as well as how to clean the fish when we got back to their house.

Also, when I went with her to get their cows in from the pasture for milking in the evening, she talked about the cows and even taught me the names of all them. She also showed me in the stable how the cows were milked and how the milk was handled. Later, in the house, she also showed me how the cream was separated from the milk and explained why they did that.

One day, when I played on an old threshing machine near the barn, I stuck my hand into a toolbox on that machine and was stung by several hornets that had a nest there that I accidentally disturbed.

The woman was very understanding when I cried, and she did something to ease the pain of the stings. When the man was told what happened to me, he was rather stern. He almost growled that I should have known better than to put my hand in that toolbox. Also, he said I *wasn't a man* when I cried after I was stung.

Also, at first, I didn't like sleeping upstairs alone. He called me a sissy about that. I told him that nobody ever slept alone upstairs at our house, but that didn't change his mind. After I slept up there alone a few times, I got used to it.

There were times, however, after I had been there for a few weeks when the man would kid around with me a little. I kind of liked that; *it made me feel more at home.*

For example, when we went to Louisburg to get fuel for his tractor, he told me that there were *streetcars* in Louisburg.

I had been in the Twin Cities, so I knew what streetcars were, and I was anxious to see what they had in Louisburg.

When we got there, I saw no more there than a gas station and a store. It didn't look like they would have streetcars.

Being a child who *believed adults,* I told the man at the gas station that I was told that there were streetcars in Louisburg. I saw that the man winked when the gas station attendant looked over toward him.

Then the man in the station said, "Well, the streetcars don't run when it's raining." It was, in fact, raining lightly at the time, but the wink made me think there was something fishy about the story; I was pretty sure they were both just kidding. I didn't mind that, since we in our family often kidded with one another.

In general, I suppose the stay with this young couple was a good experience. Also, I maybe made them more interested in having children of their own. Less than a year after I stayed with them in the summer, they adopted a boy from an orphan home in Minneapolis. A year or so later, they also adopted a little girl. I guess they got along fairly well with both of them.

I also stayed with the Max Schmeichel family for a week or two at a time, although that was not being "farmed out" like at the other place. The Schmeichel twins, Marvin and Marcia—Sonny and Sissy, as they were called—were fun to be with. They got along real well with each other and with their parents. I liked that; it was very much like it was at our house.

One time I even stayed with their family when my mom and dad and several of my brothers and sisters went to

Chicago on vacation. I guess I *asked* to stay there because our parents wouldn't have suggested it, I'm sure.

One of the reasons I may have chosen to stay with the Schmeichels at that time was that it was in September when school started. So I went to the country school with Sonny and Sis for a few days. That was a different experience for me, and it was fun to be with a few others that I knew, including Glen, Howard, and Floyd Gutzman.

I also stayed with the Gutzmans on their farm for a week or so a couple of times. That was a lot of fun because Glen was my age, and he and I got along very well.

Glen's parents—Augie Gutzman and his wife, Elsie—were good people. My folks liked them a lot, and I know they were very faithful members of the church of which my father was the pastor.

One thing I didn't like much, though, was how Glen's dad sometimes treated him. Although Glen did get into a little more monkey business than the older boys, it was almost at times as though Glen *couldn't do anything to please his dad.*

Another place I stayed for a week or so was at the farm of Henry Pansch. There, too, it wasn't like being *farmed out* either, like at the other place. Their son, Roger, was a good friend of mine.

His dad too was a fairly stern man, pretty strict. When Roger and I were playing rodeo one time with one of the calves, I thought we were in big trouble with Roger's dad, Henry. Roger and I put a rope around a calf's neck, then pulled on him, and flipped her over down on her side like the rodeo cowboys do; and something went wrong.

The calf lay on the ground, and it seemed as though it was dead. We tried our best to revive that calf, and it did no good! She was gone, we thought! Roger and I panicked! What were we to do? If that calf was dead, we were in big trouble!

We did everything to revive the calf, except to try mouth-to-mouth resuscitation. Finally, when Roger took the rope off the calf's neck and gave her a little nudge with his foot, she got up! Oh, we were so happy that the calf was still living, and we were especially happy that we weren't going to be in trouble with Roger's dad. That was the end of our trying to be rodeo cowboys.

(I mention the above incident also in the chapter of this book about raising ducks. It was while at Pansches' that I got the idea about raising ducks.)

Speaking of being "farmed out" reminds me of something else: when Manny and I were in high school, we found out that a pastor, who had been a seminary friend of our dad's, had asked Dad to let Manny and me go to live with him and his wife in Chicago, when we were about eight and ten.

According to what we were told, the friend of Dad's pleaded with him, saying that he and his wife could give us everything, including a good education. I guess they were a little more affluent than our folks, but they had no children.

We didn't care how much they could give us; we were very thankful that Dad and Mom did not even give it much thought. No matter how little our parents had, they wanted to keep us with them. *And for us, home was not a material thing; it was family.* We would not, in a million years, have traded our family or our parents for anything or anyone!

For me, being farmed out at times was enjoyable, but the best place in the world to live was *with my own family.* I thought of that so often some years later when I was attending prep school in St. Paul when I was about sixteen.

I sometimes did housework at homes near the school after classes in the afternoon. When I walked back (through snow and cold in the winter) to the dormitory for supper, I passed homes where I could see families seated at the table eating together.

Imagining being with my family in *that parsonage in little Odessa* at times like that brought tears to my eyes. Yes, I was earning something at this after-school work (probably thirty cents an hour), and I did have sufficient food at the dorm dining hall, but *it wasn't like being with my own family.*

I'm sure that it is true that home is where the heart is!

CHAPTER TEN

WILL OUR PUP BE WAITING FOR US IN HEAVEN?

W̲e had a number of pets in the parsonage while I was growing up, including several dogs. The one Manny, Danny, and I remember best was a pup called Buttons. *His life was a blessing to us, and he was fun to have with us, so what happened to him was really hard for us boys.*

Manny and I bought the dog from Davey Volgelbacher for a dollar in the summer of 1939. (I was going on eleven, Manny, nine.) We paid for the puppy with money we earned mowing lawns and doing garden work for neighbors.

Dad didn't want us to have another dog after the last one died. So we brought the pup home while Dad was in St. Paul at a pastoral conference. We thought, if we had him for several days before Dad came home, he'd let us keep him. It worked!

I don't know if Dad ever thought about how we managed that. He never said anything about it, and neither did we. I'm sure Mom knew, but she didn't say anything either. At least, we don't think she did. If she did, Dad never mentioned it to us.

Five-year-old Danny called the pup *"Buttons,"* after a dog he liked in one of his books. The name stuck. The pup was, after all, as sister Marty said, *as cute as a button.*

He was a reddish brown-and-white water spaniel with floppy ears and a stubby tail. Buttons had a wonderful personality and was very loving. When he was just months old, he'd even let my pet white pigeon Pete sit on his head.

By the end of the first summer, Buttons went with us boys almost everywhere. After he'd been with us almost a year, he even went swimming with us in the river. At the swimming hole on a bend in the Minnesota River, he was always in the water with us. The only stroke he knew was the *dog paddle,* but he did that one quite well. When he got carried away by the river current, he'd work his way over to the bank downstream and come running back.

Buttons was almost *one of the boys*. He even jumped off our raft with us, though his *cannonball* wasn't as big as ours.

One Saturday afternoon in August of 1940, we headed to the river for a swim. It was hot, and we had snipped string beans for Mom's canning project for a number of hours, so we were ready for a cool swim.

Mother asked, as we were leaving, why we didn't take our bathing suits. We told her that only *birthday suits were allowed* at the boys' swimming hole. She answered with a laugh, "I think Buttons is better dressed for swimming there than you boys." Then we all laughed.

Dad reminded me, as the oldest, to look after my brothers. He also said, "Stay away from *the spur line track!*"

"We won't go near it, Dad. Don't worry!" I replied. The Cold Spring Quarry spur line, which passed near the swimming hole, was powered by a ten-thousand-volt third rail.

Wally and Whitey Schulte came with us. It took a little longer to go by the road instead of over the school hill and through DeWaldses' pasture, but we obeyed Dad by avoiding the quarry spur line with its electric rail.

That Saturday afternoon, we five were the only ones at the swimming hole. Off came our cutoff jeans and tee shirts. No problem with shoes; all of us were barefoot.

We had a great time, swimming, diving into the river off low tree branches, and doing the "cannon ball" from the raft. Buttons was in on all the fun, and time flew by.

After a couple of hours, we saw Gordon DeWald bring his cows in. That told us that time had gone too fast! It was late! I ran and dug my pocket watch out of my pants!

"Come on, guys!" I yelled. "It's past five! Remember, I've got to ring the church bells at six!"

After we got ready to leave, I said to my brothers as I looked at my watch again, "We're gonna have to cross the spur line and go over the hill, or I won't make it to ring the bells on time!"

The boys were in disbelief, wondering if I was really going to disobey Dad. "You guys won't tell, will you?" I asked Manny and Danny. "We'll be real careful. *I've got to ring those bells right at six!* You know some people set their clocks by it!"

Although a little nervous, they nodded, and we left. We cautiously crawled under the guard fence and were very careful in crossing the tracks. We didn't really know if the electric rail was on or not, but we had to be careful, in case it was.

As we started up the school hill, I turned toward my brothers and said, wiping my brow, "Well, we all made it." All of a sudden, Danny said, "Where's Buttons?" We looked around! He wasn't with us!

At that same time, we heard the creaking of the electric flatcar, heavy with blocks of granite. That told us *the electric track was on!*

We ran back the couple of hundred feet to the guard fence! There, on the other side of the fence, we saw Buttons, trotting happily on the ties between the railroad tracks. We yelled for him to go back, but he kept coming when he saw us!

The flatcar was still out of sight around the bend as we crawled back under the fence. Buttons came toward us, stepping over the rail and the third rail.

We thought he'd made it, but his wet fur must have touched the third rail with the ten thousand volts! One shrill yelp, and he lay lifeless *over the electric rail!*

When we scrambled up the bank to the tracks, Manny and Danny dived down to take the limp pup off the rail. "Don't touch him!" I shouted excitedly. *"Don't touch him!"*

"But he's hurt," cried Danny.

"He's dead!" I yelled. "And you'll die too if you touch him!" I grabbed Danny by the arm and pushed Manny away from the deadly rail! I didn't want to hurt my brothers, but they were in grave danger, and it was my fault! I pushed Manny with my bare foot farther down the railroad bank and almost threw Danny down with him!

Then, with a stick, Wally and I got the dog off the electric rail.

Down in the weeds, we all cried and hugged the lifeless but still-warm body of our dear friend.

The flatcar of granite passed slowly by, near where we were, in the tall weeds. The men on the railcar had no idea, I'm sure, of the drama that had just taken place.

We sobbed uncontrollably over Buttons. Suddenly, I realized I still had to get to the church to ring the bells! We didn't want to leave Buttons, but we had to!

We ran over the hill and down into the village. Wally and Whitey, knowing that there'd be a bad scene over my disobeying Dad, ran on to their house.

We made it to the church and up into the bell tower just in time to ring the bells to mark *the Saturday-evening six o'clock hour*.

After we rang the bells, Manny and I jumped on the ropes to stop them. Before we got off the ropes, little brother Danny pulled the *toll bell* rope, sounding *two gongs*.

"Why'd you do that?" I asked Danny. "Dad's going to think we're foolin' around!" Little Danny sobbed, "But Buttons was just two years old, you know."

Sure enough, in a minute we heard Dad come into the church and up the steps to the balcony and bell tower. He looked angry, but when he saw us crying near the bell tower door, he asked me what was up.

I told him, although I was sobbing so uncontrollably that I almost couldn't get the words out. He listened but was very disappointed that I had disobeyed him. When he had heard the whole story, he wiped a few tears from his eyes too, and he said, kind of choked up, that he was thankful none of us was hurt.

After Dad related to Mom at the parsonage door what had happened down by the river, he told us to get a shovel and said he would go with us to bury Buttons's body.

It seemed like the walk back to the river took forever. We held each other's hand on both sides of Dad and said almost nothing.

Dad didn't say much either, except to remind me a couple times that this wouldn't have happened if I'd obeyed him.

Finally, we arrived and sadly dug a grave for Buttons. Danny picked a few wild sunflower blossoms and pushed their stems into the loose dirt on the grave.

As we clung to Dad and wept again, Dad said a prayer for us, thanking the Lord for the joy Buttons had brought to us in his short life. Also, our father asked God for forgiveness for my disobedience but thanked the Lord for helping me keep my brothers from injury or death.

There was almost total silence as we trudged up the school hill to go home. Before descending into the village on the other side of the hill, we stopped for a moment so Dad could catch his breath.

As we stood there on the edge of the hill, we could see, about a quarter of a mile away, the steeple on the church next to our house. The cross on the steeple seemed to point above the trees, toward heaven.

Danny, with his hand in Dad's, looked up and whimpered, "Father, will Buttons be waiting for us when we get to heaven?"

CHAPTER ELEVEN

JAY GOULD'S CARNIVAL COMES TO ODESSA!

It was unusual for a carnival to come to a village of three hundred inhabitants, but *Jay Gould's Million-Dollar Spectacle* did come to little Odessa in the summer of 1938.

It wasn't even a celebration or anniversary of anything in our small town. Maybe the carnival company was just filling in their schedule with an extra weekend; I don't know. I just know they came to Odessa when I was ten years old.

We didn't care why they came; we were just happy they came to our town to bring a little extra excitement. Also, it brought a lot of folks to Odessa, from all over west-central Minnesota and the adjoining counties in eastern South Dakota and southeastern North Dakota.

The carnival set things up right on *the main streets of town*. In fact, a stage and kind of a *circus ring* was set up in the middle of the street between a grain elevator and Kollitz's store and the post office.

There was no big-top tent; the stage and circus ring were right out in the open. You could actually see the stage and ring performances from the street. If you wanted to sit down, though, like most of the people did, it cost a dime for a chair in the audience rows.

One problem for the carnival people was the need for water. Odessa had no water system at that time, so all water had to be pumped from local private wells, and of course there were no public restrooms.

People who lived near downtown and the storekeepers let folks use their outdoor privies. Some of the carnival folks camped on our church lawn and used the church school outhouse. No one capitalized on anybody's need to go; I mean, they didn't charge anything. Folks in Odessa were nice that way. I guess you could say that they had an interest in people and a respect for nature.

My brother Manny and I and some other boy, capitalized on the carnival folks' need for water, though, in one way. We asked two cents for each bucket of water we carried for the animals they used in the shows.

Some boys could carry two buckets at a time. Manny and I, at eight and ten, were a little smaller; we carried one bucket together, so we each made a penny for a pail of water.

Every penny we earned was precious because most of the rides and games cost ten cents. We spent all we earned at the carnival, so they got their money back and then some.

We loved the rides, but in our opinion, *most of the games were a gyp*. We tried shooting the cork gun at prizes, but the guns didn't shoot straight. In all the games, it was difficult to win—at least anything worthwhile. The prizes a person could win were cheap things, but a lot of folks played just to have fun, so they didn't mind.

The best places to eat were *the stands* set up by the ladies' groups from the two churches. They had the best hamburgers, and they only cost a dime. The homemade root beer and sassafras were a nickel a mug, and they were great. The pop was even kept cold with blocks of ice.

We didn't see all the sideshows, but there was one we really liked. It had a real nice black man who showed people how he could do just about everything *although he was born without arms.*

Though he had no arms or hands, the man did everything using his feet; he could even scratch his ears, brush his teeth, blow his nose, comb his hair, and do a lot of other things. It was interesting to watch him.

He also had a great sense of humor along with what he said and did. When he sat down and talked with the people, he'd sometimes put one leg around his neck. That looked a little crazy, but it was natural for him.

One morning, when the man without arms didn't have much to do, Manny and I talked with him outside the tent where he did his show. He was real nice to us and thought it was interesting that we were preacher's kids because he was a Christian and liked to talk about it.

He told us that he felt that *God made him to be special* in order to show people how to live, no matter how they were made. It was an inspiration to listen to him.

One time he even *"folded" his feet* and prayed with us. Manny and I had tears in our eyes when he did that. You should have heard that prayer! He even prayed for people who had both arms and hands, asking the Lord to help them use whatever they had to His glory.

There was one sideshow where they would not allow kids. That was the one where the barker chanted over and over something like this: "See this beautiful creature the way she was born, so ask your father for a quarter! He'll want to come see her too. She's dressed real pretty—in the outfit she had on when she was born—her birthday suit."

I didn't know what that was about; I didn't even know why he said the same dumb thing over and over. Then Eddie Thole told me. He knew more about some things than I did, even though he was less than a year older than I.

Manny and I still couldn't figure out why guys would put down twenty-five cents of their hard-earned money to see a woman dressed in her birthday suit. But then, not all people think the same way.

Speaking of barkers, there was one who tried to get attention for a sideshow one day by auctioning off what he said was *"a crisp new dollar bill."*

"Step right up, ladies and gentlemen, boys and girls," he would say over and over, "and make your bid on this crisp new dollar bill!"

At first nobody bid on it; they were pretty sure it was counterfeit, because *it looked too crisp and too new.* Finally, ten-year-old Donavan Will bid a nickel. The barker tried and tried to get more bids, but that's all he got. He finally called out, "Going, going, gone! This dollar bill is sold to this boy for five cents!"

As Donavan stepped forward timidly, several guys hissed, "Sucker! You're gonna get a crumby worthless piece of paper you can blow your nose in for your nickel!"

Donavan was cross-eyed, but he had his head on straighter than a lot of guys. When the barker asked for his nickel, Donavan fumbled in his pocket, then pulled his hand out with a nickel in it. Eying his nickel one more time, he clutched it in his fist, looked up at the man, and said, "Why don'cha just take the five cents out of the dollar and give me the change?" Pretty smart; huh? That was Donavan!

I learned another bit of wisdom at the carnival from the MC at the afternoon show. He called out one day over the speaker, "Folks, a purse was just found by Helen Hunt!"

When everybody was listening pretty well, he called out, "The person who lost that purse can go to Helen Hunt for it!" A lot of people laughed; Manny and I didn't know why they laughed till Eddie Thole told us about that too. I don't think Eddie was smarter than we were; he just caught on like an adult sometimes.

One kind of sad thing during the carnival days was when one of the town's Grain Belt lovers set up in an alley, charging people to throw raw eggs at him as he stuck his face through an old bedsheet.

Believe it or not, quite a few guys, including a couple baseball players from Ortonville, took him up on it, for five cents an egg. He sure got smashed in the face enough times, but that was what he was charging guys to do.

It didn't seem right to smash good eggs in a man's face. But I guess some fellows got enjoyment out of hittin' the guy in the kisser with what chickens had produced as food for us. And the man who stuck his face out, watching the raw eggs come at him, made enough, I guess, to buy some more of his favorite refreshment.

Not all of the Jay Gould's carnival was wholesome entertainment for preacher's sons, but we boys, like a lot of folks in Big Stone County and surrounding area, did have some special fun for a few days.

Of course, we PKs (preacher's kids) could also extend our education by learning a few things from more experienced friends, even friends not much older than we were.

And we could buy tasty hamburgers and real refreshing mugs of root beer while at the same time contributing to a good cause.

CHAPTER TWELVE

THE BRIDE AND GROOM JUST *DISAPPEARED!*

Our pastor father officiated at many weddings in the congregations he served in western Minnesota. Most of those weddings were large affairs, especially those that involved German farm families.

One of the German words for wedding is *Hochzeit,* which literally translated is "high time." And it surely was a *high time* for the families! Our brother Vernon joked that there was another reason "high time" was used for a wedding. He said if the girl was almost twenty-five years old, her parents thought it was *high time she got married,* or she would be an old maid. That was Vernon's idea; I'm not sure it was that way.

The family of the bride usually decorated the church, and they always *dressed up* the whole place in a special way. Also, the bride, groom, and the wedding party wore their finest. The bride's gown and the dresses of her bridesmaids and attendants were usually personally sewn by someone in the bride's family.

The men didn't usually wear tuxedos, but they were always *spiffied up* in good-looking suits, new for the occasion, bought at JCPenney's or some other special place.

It seemed like everybody and his brother were invited to the weddings from all over Big Stone County and other parts of Minnesota and South Dakota. Often, more people showed up at the reception than at the wedding ceremony at the church. Maybe some came just for the food and drinks of all kinds. There was always plenty of everything!

These farm families really knew how to celebrate! The family spared nothing, it seemed, especially when a daughter got married. If *Hochzeit* was a *high time*, it applied more to the reception than to the wedding itself. They *killed the fatted calf* for the wedding dinner and anything else they needed from the farm!

One of the weddings in the summer of 1938 was really a big affair. I was not quite ten at that time, and Manny was a few months from eight. There were more people at the wedding ceremony and at the reception on the farm than I had ever seen before! In this case, the bride and the groom were both from large German farm families in the Odessa area.

Our family was invited, of course. Manny and I had a great time playing with the boys, even though most of them were a little older than we were.

After we played for a while, we went inside. Something strange happened at this reception after the dinner. At least brother Manny and I thought it was strange. In the middle of it all, *the bride and groom disappeared!*

After the opening of the many gifts and having the big dinner, with all the serious and "not so serious" speeches, the bride (the farmer's daughter) and the groom went upstairs. People thought they went up there to change clothes or something, but they never came down; at least no one saw them. It seemed that they just vanished into thin air!

How could they disappear? And if they did, where did they go? And holy smoke, *why would they want to leave the celebration?* It seemed that the festivities were just getting under way, but just like that, the bride and groom were nowhere to be seen!

Soon the bride's teenage brother and a few other boys, including our fourteen-year-old brother, Vernon, set out to look for them, like they thought they got lost or something.

The boys figured, I guess, that the bride and groom were somewhere on the farm because the groom's shiny black '33 Ford was still there. Manny and I followed along with the boys, but we couldn't figure out what was really happening.

The party was in honor of the bride and groom; why would they leave? And if there was something wrong, why were the boys all laughing while they were looking for them?

And the places they looked! We couldn't figure that out either. With flashlights, the boys looked in the hay maw in the barn, in the tack room, and in the corncrib. They even looked in every nook and cranny in the grove on the north side of the house. Then they spread out and walked through one of the cornfields near the farm buildings.

Manny and I sure wondered why the boys chuckled and laughed while they looked for the bride and groom. They acted like all this was funny, but Manny and I thought, if those two were lost out in the dark or something, why was this so humorous?

And for that matter, if the bride and groom wanted to be by themselves for a while, away from the crowd, why didn't those boys just leave them alone?

We asked one of the boys what was funny about this, and he said, "You little kids don't know nothin', do you?" When the boy ran away again to join the other boys, I said to Manny, "We aren't as big as he is, but I know we do better in school than he does. How does he figure that we're dumb?"

Of course, when I thought about it, it wasn't too hard for anybody to do better in school than that boy did! However, it bothered me that he and the other guys knew something that we didn't and didn't want to tell us.

Of course, I knew that those boys had gotten into a jug of homemade wine before dinner, so I thought they were all a little silly. But when I told Manny, he said somebody said that it was dandelion wine. "And," he added, "how could anything made from little yellow flowers make anybody silly?"

Later, when we were called by sister Marcia to get ready to leave for home, Manny and I asked Vernon about the mystery. He just chuckled, shook his head, and told us that we were too little to understand such things. "Maybe one day you'll be old enough to understand," he said to us. We wondered why Vernon thought he was so smart.

I wanted to ask Marty if she knew what this was all about, but I sure didn't want to hear *a girl* tell us that *we were dumb*, so we just got into the car and let the matter go while Dad drove us home.

We never did find out what happened to the bride and groom that night. Mom and Dad didn't say anything about it, but we thought maybe they weren't even aware of the couple's disappearance. And neither Vernon nor Marty said a word about it that night or anytime.

Manny and I tried to forget about the whole thing, but it still was a mystery to us. We didn't ask anyone about it, though, any more.

The next Sunday we saw both the bride and the groom in church, and they both looked just fine. They smiled at each other and at other people, like nothing had happened. They just seemed *like happy newlyweds*.

Manny and I concluded that whatever happened the night of their wedding couldn't have been too serious, so we didn't say any more about it to anyone.

CHAPTER THIRTEEN

MY FIRST BIKE—
A TWO-DOLLAR INVESTMENT

My first bicycle really did cost two dollars. Brother Ihno got it for me from a professor's son at Concordia College in St. Paul in June of 1940. It wasn't in great shape, but it was my primary means of transportation for several years.

The bike was brought, *all apart*, on the top of a '32 Model A Ford in which Ihno rode home from college with fellow students from Milbank, South Dakota. The bike needed a lot of work; even the wheels had to be partly respoked.

Davey Volgebacher, who had some experience with bikes, helped me get the bike running. The bike was high for me, but I managed to ride it with the seat down on the frame as far as it would go.

The first thing I did when we got the bicycle going was to ride over to the Gloeges to see if Clarence was still interested in selling his paper route. He said he was; his price was $1.25, and I couldn't get him down any below that, no matter how hard I tried.

I couldn't afford that much, but he said he'd take fifty cents down and three weekly payments of two bits each. Dad gave me permission to do it, if I'd pay him myself. Dad showed me his empty billfold saying he wasn't able to help me or float me a loan.

After I made the deal with Clarence and the *Minneapolis Star-Journal* okayed me as one of their carriers, I was in business. To start, I had eighteen homes and three businesses as customers. They were spread out over the whole town about four miles round-trip.

In the summer, I could use my bike, and it was usually daylight when I made my round. In the winter, because of the snow, I had to walk, and it was usually dark and often colder than a walk-in freezer in the whole town.

One place I didn't like going in the dark was the Odessa train depot. There were usually a couple hobos sleeping on the floor. It was hard to see in there at night, so occasionally I'd stumble over one and get cussed out, especially if the guy was *three sheets to the wind*. However, nobody ever hurt me, and I had heard most of the language those guys used, only in a theological sense.

I tried to witness for the Lord to one of the hobos who cussed me out one evening. When I said to him, as I was going out the door, "God loves you, you know, and sent Jesus to be your Savior," he gave me a nicely engraved card that said,

Dear friend, you are cordially invited to the place of eternal punishment.

I think I still have that card. I had never been told to *go to hell* on a nicely engraved card before.

Dad smiled when he saw it, but as my father and pastor, he suggested that I disregard it. In fact, Dad said, with a smile, "By all means, do not feel you have to respond to that invitation." Then Dad said, "Remind me tonight when we have devotion to pray for that man."

That incident reminded me of a time a hobo came to the parsonage for a handout. (That was almost a daily occurrence at the parsonage, especially in summer.) Before Dad fed him on the back steps, he gave the hobo some wood to chop so he would feel as though he had earned his lunch. As always, Dad sat with him as he ate and gave the man *a little Law and Gospel* while the man was eating.

According to Dad, the man pointed to holes in his overalls and said, "Reverend, I gotta tell ya that my pants is wore out in the knees from prayin' so much." Dad told the man that it was good that he prayed.

Then, with a smile, the hobo said, "An' ya know why it's wore out in the seat of my pants?" Before Dad could answer, the man with the tattered backside said, "From backslidin'! Yes, sir, from backslidin', Rever'nd."

I guess Dad had a hard time keeping from laughing, but I think he still gave him a blessing when he left and reminded him that God loved him.

Back to the newspapers. There were no leash laws in Odessa, so almost all the dogs ran loose. Fortunately, I knew most of them, but I had problems with one man's pack of five or six pups one time. They especially liked to chase after my bike.

I saw the man who owned the dogs one day and told him about the problem. The man, who'd had a few too many beers when I talked to him, simply said, "Just kick those little—s! That'll teach 'em!"

The next day I did what the man told me, and those aggressive pups *didn't like it at all!* They almost tore me off my bike. I think I still have a few marks on my legs where they nabbed me. My brother Vernon, who was home from prep school at the time that happened, said, "The problem was, when those dogs went after you, and you kicked them, you didn't use the same language the man used in referring to them."

My reply to Vernon was, "Maybe, but even though I know what *a female dog is called*, how did I know if they were all *sons?* Some may have been daughters." He had to think a little about what I said. Mom even laughed at that one as she cleaned up my wounds and put on some medication.

The customers on my paper route paid fifteen cents for the six dailies and seven cents for the Sunday paper at that time (in 1940).

Some people always had the twenty-two cents ready on Saturday when I came to collect. A few even gave me a quarter and told me to keep the three cents change; that was nice.

When I made a little extra like that, I could buy another stamp or two for my collection of *"little windows of history,"* as I called the postage stamps in my collection.

There were a few customers, however, who were more full of promises about paying than the Minnesota River was with thorny-headed bullheads.

The *Star-Journal* didn't want us to "carry" customers who didn't pay on time, but what could a preacher's kid do? Some of the customers were Dad's parishioners, so I always thought I had to be careful what I said to them.

One man told me when I gave him his paper *as he was coming out of a bar* one day, "You're a—good kid. I'm gonna give you a quarter at Christmastime." He said that in early December.

Needless to say, when I collected for the paper just before Christmas, I waited after he paid me the regular amount, but all I got after that was a grunted "thank you and Merry Christmas" in Swedish. At least, I think that's what he said.

My sister Marty said the guy was probably telling me in his language, "Sorry, kid. See, *I'd had a few* the day I made the promise of a tip. Today I'm sober." Maybe Marty was right.

My commission was supposed to be about $1.60 a week. That wasn't too bad, but I still thought I'd rather become a preacher when I grew up, even if it didn't pay that much more.

CHAPTER FOURTEEN

MY MOST HUMILIATING MOMENT

*Preacher's kids are supposed to be
quiet in church.*

The most humiliating moment of my life was when I was sent home from church by my pastor father one Sunday morning *in the middle of his sermon*. It was a beautiful day in western Minnesota till that moment. When Dad told me to go home, there was the darkest cloud over my head that I had ever experienced.

Well, maybe it wasn't the most humiliating moment of my life up to the time I'm writing this, but it was surely the most humiliating moment of my life up to that Sunday morning when I was about ten years old. It must have been in spring of 1939.

I'm writing this in December of 2007; about six weeks ago, I celebrated my seventy-ninth birthday. Now, when I say "celebrated," maybe that isn't the right word. When we get this old, usually we just *observe* our birthdays. We don't really *celebrate* them; right? We've had so many, we aren't really that thrilled about them like we were when we were kids.

I remember well one birthday *that most assuredly was celebrated;* that was when I turned eight. My sister Adie, who was fourteen at that time, organized a birthday party for me. Maybe if the Sunday-morning black cloud had hung over my head before that, she wouldn't have arranged a celebration for my birthday.

Nevertheless, Adie did organize a party for me on my birthday in 1936. Because I was turning eight, she invited six boys so that with Manny and me we'd be eight, one for each year I had lived.

Talk about time passing, several of those boys are no longer walking the earth. Dale Woodley died when he was about ten; my cousin, Junior Mews, died when he was fifty; and my little brother Manny died in 1989, at fifty-eight.

What am I doing here yet? If I live another year, until October of 2008, I'll hit the "big eighty (80)!" Isn't that something?! Maybe, although I'm a fervent believer, the Lord just hasn't decided what to do with me. After all, I one time ruffled my father's feathers so seriously that he sent me home from church *right in the middle of his sermon*!

I think I was sent home from church by Dad just as he was starting *the third part of his discourse.* And I do remember that he was preaching in English, which was a little more difficult for him since his native tongue was German.

One thing I remember well, though, was that when Dad decided—*on the spur of the moment,* I'm sure—to send me down that aisle of the church to the door, he switched from English to German faster than a rattlesnake here in Arizona can strike when it's coiled and ready!

I don't know how Dad got himself back into the English language after his *momentary Germanic explosion* that spring Sunday morning. It must have been that he happened to glance at Art Hoerneman, a nice boy who was a star pupil in his confirmation class that year. Maybe Art's smiling face at that moment seemed to be saying, "English only, please, Pastor. I'm taking notes on your sermon for our confirmation class."

I know for sure, though, that when Dad told me in no uncertain terms to go home from church, without my hearing the third part of his discourse, *the words did come out in German!*

Those gruff words had to come out in German! English just doesn't have the same guttural sounds that explode from the throat and spring from the epiglottis to gritted teeth and quivering lips *like German does!*

If any of you who read this are given to sudden explosions of anger like my father experienced *on my account* that spring Sunday morning in 1939, *learn German*! It's the ideal language for expressing anger, especially if one of your kids *has put a match to your wick.*

However, please don't misunderstand me. *Ich liebe dich* (I love you) said at the right time, in the right place, can melt a girl's heart. On the other hand, you could get slapped if you call her "honeybunch" in German. (Somehow, *honigklumpen* just doesn't seem to be the thing to whisper in a girl's ear. If you'd call her *honigklumpen'*, she'd think you'd lost your senses, or she may even charge you with abuse.)

At this point, I have to tell any of you people who know folks who have lived in Odessa what happened the last time brother Vernon and I visited the little village. There was no special occasion. We were just passing through; it must have been about 1998. (Don't get too nervous; this has a tie-in with my getting sent home from church.)

Vern and I were having a cup of coffee at the Mudhen Restaurant in downtown Odessa with our spouses, talking about old times. We were the only ones in the restaurant at that time—in the middle of the afternoon. When the manager heard us talking about Odessa, he came over to where we were sitting and said, "It sounds like you fellows grew up here in Odessa."

When we said yes and told him that we grew up in the Trinity Lutheran parsonage, he asked if we knew LeRoy Strei. We said, "Yes, of course." After hearing our answer, he asked his son to get LeRoy from his house nearby. LeRoy was about eighty-five at that time, but as alive as he ever was and had a sense of humor like he had when he was young.

LeRoy came over to the restaurant, and we had *a wonderful, hilarious two hours together with him.* I wouldn't doubt it if Vernon and LeRoy are continuing the enjoyable conversation today in eternity since they've both gone on before us.

Now comes the tie-in with my humiliating moment in 1939: I asked LeRoy that day in Odessa in 1998 if he remembered when I was sent out of church one Sunday morning in 1939 just as Dad was beginning the third part of his discourse.

Believe it or not, *he did remember*! In fact, he said he could recall how a few of the old Germans, *on the men's side*, turned around to watch me go down the aisle, following me with their stern German eyeballs with a look of satisfaction as I took slow steps toward the door with my head down in humiliation.

LeRoy said he had wondered all these years what got Dad's dander up like that two-thirds of the way through his sermon just as he was starting the third part of his discourse. Well, I told LeRoy what it was that upset Dad that day.

When I tried to convince LeRoy that Manny and Danny were more at fault than I, he didn't believe me, though he had a pretty good laugh over it. Actually, Vernon and our wives didn't believe me either. They too had a good laugh over the whole thing.

So why should I tell you? You see, one of the problems I've always had was that I too often had a look on my face like *the cat that ate the canary*. Maybe that's what Dad saw when he looked at me that morning. *(See the picture of me as a kid of that age in the photo section of this book.)*

By the way, LeRoy got the last and best laugh that day at the Odessa Mudhen when he asked, "What is a discourse, anyway?"

CHAPTER FIFTEEN

TWENTY YEARS OF JANSSENS IN THE ODESSA SCHOOL

*Reading and writing and 'rithmetic taught to
the tune of the hickory stick . . .*

The Odessa Public School (all twelve grades in one building) stood on a hill on the south side of the village. I say "stood" (past tense) because there is nothing but a vacant lot there today.

Although I am near the Mexican border in Arizona, as I am writing this in 2007, *I can hear the many children in the schoolyard of District 24 in Odessa, playing ball, hopscotch, and jumping rope or just chatting with one another* on a pleasant spring morning, waiting for the bell to ring to start another day of classes.

It's depressing to see nothing but grass on *the school hill* today. That building identified Odessa like the Sears Tower identifies Chicago. It is sad that it is gone from the face of the earth! It's like the village has had its heart removed.

The Odessa school was alive and well during the years our family lived in Odessa. Interestingly, the school was not without a member of our family during all those years, 1927 to 1947!

When our family arrived in Odessa from Wisconsin in February of 1927, Ihno and Ruth were in fourth grade, and Anita was in first. *More were to come!* At home, still underfoot in 1927, were Adie, age five; Vern, three; and Marty, one.

Only the Lord knew that *I* was scheduled to come (*born in that very parsonage*, with the help of Ortonville's Dr. Shelver) in 1928. I was number 7, the first of the Janssen siblings born in Odessa.

Manny and Danny followed later, and Danny was still attending that school in eighth grade when our parents pulled stakes for Wisconsin in 1947.

When I started first grade in 1934, there were *seven of us Trinity Lutheran PKs* (preacher's kids) in the school. I wonder if there was any family in the community that had more than seven in that school at the same time!

That school year, 1934-'35, Ihno and Ruth were seniors in high school, Anita was in ninth grade, Adie in seventh, Vernon in fifth, Marty in third, and I was in first. What a lineup! Almost every teacher had a Janssen for a pupil! (They'd maybe groan at the thought.)

I'll never forget my first day of school in Odessa. I had convinced our mother that I should wear my Sunday-go-meetin'-clothes red corduroy overalls.

I didn't tell Mother why I wanted to wear my neat red corduroys; I was sure she wouldn't understand. Actually,

I wanted to wear the best clothes I had in the hope that I could impress Lorna Mae Stegner, a lovely girl I knew who was going to be in my class.

Lorna was about the prettiest girl I'd ever seen—and I'd already lived almost six long years! I'd seen a lot, no?

Needless to say, *I did not impress Lorna.* The disappointment was short-lived, however, because I became enamored with the teacher, Ms. Aamodt. I remember that when I went home for lunch at noon that day, I told our mother that Ms. Aamodt was almost as nice as *my mother.* Mom probably smiled at the thought.

I'm sure that the "feeling" I had for Ms. Aamodt was not mutual, though. Instead of her thinking that I was a nice kid, she must have thought I was a pain *you-know-where.*

You see, sister Marty, two years older than I, was in the same room—she in third grade, I in first. Marty went home each day and reported on the day's happenings—not always the best for me.

Of course, one of the reasons I frustrated the teacher was Marty's fault. When she was in first grade, she came home from school each day and made me, at age four, her *homeschool pupil.*

Marty taught me, to the best of her ability, everything she had learned from her teacher. So when I started in first grade, I was able to read and was acquainted with all the stories used with first graders; I butted in constantly, telling her what my sister Marty had taught me when she was in first grade.

I'm sure that I frustrated her more than any other kid in our class—even more than my cousin, Junior Mews, who also gave the teacher a pain *where she couldn't get a pill.*

Marty always got home in the afternoon before I did and told Mom and Dad everything that happened that day in school. So *I suffered double jeopardy*—getting bawled out by Ms. Aamodt in school and hearing a barrage of German from Dad at home. He never could speak English when he was angry, which at me was too often, I'm sorry to say. I wasn't a bad kid; I just ruffled teachers' feathers by talking too much.

I didn't mean for this chapter to go in this direction, but I do remember another teacher whose feathers I inadvertently ruffled. Her name was Ms. Anderson—a young teacher, but more clever than some old pros. This happened when I was in about fifth grade (1938).

As my cousin Erich Mews was giving a talk in class one day, I sat in the back of the room, making faces at him. (The teacher was sitting facing the speaker, so she couldn't see me.) When I made faces at Erich, he started to laugh; then he cried!

The teacher asked Erich what was wrong, and he whimpered, "Arlo is making faces at me." Wow, he had to be *so truthful at that moment*, which Erich wasn't always!

I was asked to stay after school. Knowing this teacher was no one's fool, I feared what was going to happen when I'd meet with her alone after school, *with no audience.*

When just the two of us met after school, she asked if indeed I had made faces at Erich while he was giving his talk in front of the class. How could I deny it? I said, as humbly as I could, with my head down, "Yes, I did. I'm sorry."

Then Ms. Anderson said, "Show me what you did when Erich was giving his talk." I must have looked pretty bewildered as she went on. "Please, make some faces at me right now, like you made at Erich in the class." I was dumbfounded! Then *I cried!*

Incidentally, I used that story a few times when I was teaching speech communications classes at Cochise College here in Arizona. What Ms. Anderson did and said there in Odessa decades earlier was an interesting lesson for my students who were giving talks to their friends! They laughed when I told them the story, but I think it helped them respect each other when speaking in front of the class.

There's one more bit of wisdom I learned at the Odessa school with regard to discipline. That was from A. E. Pagel, the Odessa school superintendent when I was in eighth or ninth grade.

Any of you who went to Odessa school when A. E. Pagel was in charge, remember that the man's sunken eyes under his shiny, hairless pate were an extension of his no-nonsense, stern superintendent's brain. Those eyes could penetrate steel; of that, I am quite confident!

At that time (1943?), it was the style for girls to wear black—especially black skirts and sweaters. That color was an invitation for the boys to make white "designs" on their clothes with chalk erasers. The favorite was for one boy to make an imprint on a girl's back with the chalk eraser and another to cross it to make an *X*.

Wallace Schulte and I, one morning, armed with concealed weapons (well-used erasers full of chalk dust), walked up the stairs behind Mabel Pansch. As she reached the top of the stairs, Wallace "accidentally" bumped her, making the first mark on Mabel who was sharply dressed in her black skirt and sweater. I followed with another "nudge," completing the *X* on the lower part of her back.

Mission accomplished; right? Wrong! Mr. Pagel was nearby, in the door to the library, and witnessed my completing Wallace's *X signature!* I was caught "white-handed!" Wallace had *not been seen* making his mark.

You never saw a more innocent look on Wallace's face as when Mr. Pagel apprehended me for my *chalk art*. Wallace stood there with a look on his face that indicated that he was saying inside, "Shame on you, Arlo. How could you do a thing like that?"

Unfortunately (for me!), Mr. Pagel and my father, the Reverend Ihno Janssen, were friends. Mr. Pagel knew that Dad had methods of dealing with his kids on which a superintendent could not improve! So *I was sent home! In the middle of the morning, I was sent home!*

It must have taken me a half hour to walk the few blocks to our house. At home, I found out that Mr. Pagel had already called my parents, so all I could do was plead guilty. Our parents weren't violent people, but sometimes I wished they had used their hands more.

The three-part sermon discourse in German I got that day was more painful in some respects than a hand application would have been where the Creator had divided my posterior!

What made matters infinitely worse was that this was the day before Thanksgiving. *The aforementioned Reverend Ihno Janssen was scheduled to speak to the school assembly and lead a Thanksgiving devotion* the last hour of that day!

Talk about *"holy smoke, the church is on fire!"* The fumes which arose from my father's head that morning in our house next to the church could have been used by Indians to communicate from one mountain to another! The "sentence" of restrictions pronounced on me that morning was more than I could bear—I thought!

The only advantage (if you could call it that) of hearing such a barrage of German was that I learned more of the language every time that kind of thing happened. To this day, however, I *understand* German better than I speak it, but I still get along well enough when I need to.

I didn't mean for this chapter of the book I'm writing about my growing up in a Lutheran parsonage to be *a personal confession,* but you could look at it another way: *the Odessa school personnel knew fairly well how to handle kids full of the Old Nick, including some PKs.*

PS I did not graduate from high school at Odessa. (After ten years at the Odessa school, I enrolled at Concordia Academy in St. Paul.) Had I stayed at Odessa High School, that is, if I had finished the twelfth grade, I would surely have been in the *top ten* of my graduating class—*there were* nine *graduates that year!*

CHAPTER SIXTEEN

COLLECTING LITTLE WINDOWS OF HISTORY (Postage Stamps)

In the summer of 1939, our mother and father and a few of the younger kids in the family drove from our home in Odessa, Minnesota, to Chicago, Illinois, to visit Mom's brother, the Reverend Theodore Thormahlen, and his family. Uncle Ted was the superintendent of a Lutheran orphan home in Addison, in the Chicago area.

This orphanage regularly received from individuals, churches, and other organizations more used clothing, puzzles, and games for children than the orphanage could use. Some of the extra things were given to needy families. When our parents visited there, our large family was usually given a few of those excess gifts received by the home.

I wasn't along on that vacation, so I have no idea why certain things were given to our parents. When they returned from the visit there in 1939, believe it or not, one of the things brought along was a shopping bag full of used postage stamps on paper.

There must have been thousands of used stamps in that bag—all on paper. No one in the family had ever, that I have known, had an interest in postage stamps, so the bag wasn't touched by anyone for some months.

One day, I happened on the bag and took some of the stamps out and looked at them. I noticed that most of them were from Canada. The pictures on them interested me, so I dumped some out on a bed in an upstairs bedroom and started to sort them out.

A little later, in a grade-school hobby club meeting, I mentioned that I had a bag of stamps and was trying to sort them according to countries and types of stamps.

It was a good thing I mentioned the stamps because the hobby club supervisor, Mr. Sheltens, was himself a stamp collector. He gave me a lot of suggestions about how to remove stamps from paper, how to identify countries, and how to start a collection. He also gave me the names of several stamp companies from which stamps could be purchased.

I had a paper route at that time, and I bought a few stamps now and then with money I made from delivering papers. I couldn't afford to buy a stamp album, so I made my own with two thin pieces of plywood the size of art paper pages through which I made holes with a wood-burning tool for metal rings to hold paper like a notebook. Then I printed the names of countries on pages of white art paper, copying the names of the countries from Mr. Sheltens's album.

He thought my homemade album was ingenious. It was nice to hear that kind of praise, especially from a teacher who wasn't given that much to praising his students.

Believe me, I didn't get that much praise from him in math class. To be sure, I wasn't a star student in math. My interest in stamps in a relatively short time surpassed my interest in mathematics.

Although I did buy an album a couple of years later, I kept that first album, and I still have it to this day after more than six decades. It wasn't the greatest, but now I regard it as a keepsake.

Mr. Sheltens did not stay in Odessa very long. He went back, after a year or two, to St. Paul, which I believe was his hometown.

I remember that he had one shoe that had a sole about three or four inches thick. He walked with a limp, but he never acted like he was handicapped. In fact, he helped to coach a grade-school basketball team, though I'm sure he himself had never played; I rather think he was born with one leg shorter than the other.

Although I didn't excel in Mr. Sheltens's math class, I surely appreciated what he did in getting me started in stamp collecting after I had that bag of stamps from the orphanage in Illinois.

After I enrolled in a prep school when I was fifteen years old, I didn't do much with stamps anymore although I was always interested in those *little windows of history* as I had learned to call them. A number of years went by before I became active with stamps again—maybe at least fifteen years.

In 1959, while I was living and working in Philadelphia, Pennsylvania, I quit smoking. At that time, I again became interested in stamps. I never realized it at the time, but renewing my interest in stamp collecting probably was significant in helping to overcome the habit of smoking.

I just thought at the time that I would invest in stamps about the same amount that I was spending on cigarettes, which was about ten dollars a month. I did make some good investments in stamps, but even the stamps that never appreciated in value were worth more than *burned-up cigarettes*. I could at least use them as postage.

There was something more than the worth of stamps that I developed in the years after that. In 1959 and 1960, I got involved in the People to People program which was started by President Eisenhower in the 1950s.

It was at that time that there was a tremendous struggle in the world between communism and freedom. It was President Eisenhower's idea that ordinary people could sell the ideology of freedom in the world, in some respects, better than the government of our country could. He encouraged people with special interests to write to people in other countries who had similar interests.

Representatives in the U.S. government somehow gathered lists of people in many countries with various interests. *Stamp collecting* was one of them.

It was through the People to People program that I started corresponding with stamp collectors in various countries. Over the years, it grew with some people also *contacting me*. (Where they got my name and address,

I do not know.) However, I answered all the letters I received. A few of them were even from women, usually teachers.

In a matter of a few years, I had about sixty correspondents in over forty countries of the world. I didn't type very well at that time, but I bought an old typewriter and set up a little *office* in a *spare* upstairs bedroom in our house.

Almost every evening, before I went to bed, I typed at least one letter. That way, I wrote to all them at least once every two months, even though most of them answered much sooner than that.

In this correspondence, I not only had an opportunity to spread ideas regarding freedom, but with many of them, I was able to witness for the Christian faith. In fact, a number of them were more full of questions about *the faith* than about *political ideas*.

One of them was a black missionary in Africa who wanted so much to discuss things regarding the Bible and the Christian faith. He always closed his letters with, "If I never see you here, I will surely see you hereafter." I thought that was a beautiful thought. Over the years, I've lost track of him as a correspondent, but I'm sure that *the Lord will let us meet hereafter when we are together with Him*.

Of course, there was always an *exchange of stamps* too. With most of these correspondents, we exchanged *used stamps*, so it didn't cost too much for either of us. One correspondent in a small town in Canada sent some cards and letters beautifully decorated with Canadian stamps. I still have almost all those just the way he sent them.

In the summer of 1968, I visited that man in that little town in Ontario where he operated a *corner grocery store*. Before the end of that year, I was notified that he had gone to be with the Lord. He too was a Christian, and we exchanged many ideas about the faith. I surely look forward to *seeing him* too after this life.

Stamp collecting has been a very interesting hobby for me. In effect, it has been much more than a hobby. When I was a schoolboy, teachers were very surprised that *I knew where all the countries of the world were*. That was the result of my working with stamps.

When I gave up smoking in 1959, I did not realize at first that my interest in stamps took the place of smoking—a smelly habit that had no value.

Also, I have to this day thousands of dollars worth of stamps, most of which I have stored for safekeeping. Some have appreciated in value, and *all can be at least be used for postage*. In fact, through my using older stamps for postage, I know I have gotten some other people interested in stamps.

Also, the exchange of thoughts, ideas, and stamps with many people around the world has been an education and a very valuable interest for me. I know it was of value too for the many international correspondents I had over the years. It truly was a *people to people* experience.

I would recommend that type of experience for anyone. To be sure, much can also be learned from stamps. They are truly *little windows of history*. In fact, for me they have been *windows through which I have seen more of the world*.

CHAPTER SEVENTEEN

RUTH AND IHNO—
THE FIRSTBORN JANSSENS

Ruth and Ihno were the firstborn in our family. Not only were they the first in that they were the oldest, but they also were the first to help each other further their education, something most of us in our large family did also. They helped each other when there was need. Let me first tell you a little about the first two of the Janssen siblings.

When the folks moved with the family to Odessa in February of 1927, Ruth and Ihno were ten and nine. However, there were already four more children in the family besides Ruth and Ihno Junior for a total of six children in eleven years of our parents' marriage.

They had to wait until the family had been in Odessa for about a year and a half before I showed up. I was born in October of 1928—*number 7* of the siblings, the first of the Janssen family born in Odessa.

I wonder what the people in the Trinity congregation in Odessa thought when the new pastor arrived in 1927. "Have you heard?" a lady in the congregation may have said to a friend. "The new pastor has six children, and the oldest is only ten! Poor Mrs. Janssen, with all those little ones!

If Minnie, the mother of those six, would have heard what was said, she may well have wanted to say to them, "Yes, we have six, and we think maybe the Lord will give us more—who knows, maybe four more. My pastor husband says *we don't have money to support any children,* and if my teacher's math is right, *ten times nothing is still nothing!"*

"But then," Minnie might have wanted to go on to say, "who knows, the Lord may choose a few of these *little ones* to someday become pastors, teachers, or other kinds of Christian workers for the world. Only the Lord knows."

The first two of the ten children born to Pastor Ihno and his wife, Minnie, did indeed grow up to be a pastor and a Christian schoolteacher. Ruth was also a good pianist and church organist. Ihno not only became a parish pastor, but also a district and synodical official in the Lutheran Church.

But I shouldn't get ahead of myself. A lot occurred before Ihno and Ruth became what our parents always hoped they would be. And *how can I* get ahead of anything? *I, the seventh Janssen little one, didn't meet* Ruth and Ihno Junior until they were in the middle of elementary school!

I do not know much of Ruth and Ihno's growing-up years, since they were seniors in high school in the 1934-35 school year when I was in first grade. It's hard for me to imagine, but I was just going on seven *when they graduated from high school!*

Ruth and Ihno both played basketball in high school; that I remember. As a little kid, I was taken to some of their games. The games were played in the old town hall, which was near the church and parsonage in Odessa. (The *new town hall,* a masterpiece built by the WPA, was completed in 1936, a year after Ruth and Ihno graduated.)

Both Ruth and Ihno said that when they entered school in Odessa in February of 1927 in the fourth grade, the other children were a little cool toward them.

Who knows why the children were not friendly toward them at first. Maybe it was because *everybody knew everybody* in a little town like Odessa, and these were *the new kids* not known by anybody. Also, some kids may have said, "They're preacher's kids. They think they're something special!" Furthermore, the kids from our family were entering school *in the middle of the year.* That probably didn't happen often in Odessa.

Ihno told me that one boy who did invite him, ever so timidly, to play with him was Bruno Schwandt. It's interesting that Ihno and Bruno Schwandt—later, a restaurant owner and operator in Appleton, Minnesota— remained friends and are to this today.

Ihno and Bruno are still in contact—these eighty years later, though they live nearly two thousand miles apart (Bruno in Appleton, Minnesota, and Ihno in San

Francisco)! Both are today (in 2008) nearly ninety years old and still getting along fairly well for their age.

I guess the *coolness* in the Odessa school was short-lived, however, because it didn't take Ruth and Ihno long to become very much involved in school activities and community life. That was especially true in their high school years.

Both Ruth and Ihno were active in sports and other activities. Also, Ihno formed a male quartette in high school, and Ruth was their accompanist. The quartette was made up of Gerhardt Schwandt, Art Stock, Ihno, and LeRoy Strei; it was called the GAIL Quartette, an acronym formed from the first letters of their first names. The GAIL Quartette sang at many occasions over the years at school as well as in church (they were all members of Trinity) and at community functions.

Incidentally, Ruth and Ihno were not twins, although they were in the same grade through most of their school years. In Mattoon, Wisconsin, where the family had previously lived, Ihno was advanced a grade (from first to third, skipping second) in the small school they attended.

When I asked Ihno how he happened to skip a grade, believe it or not, he said, as far as he knows, they were trying to even up the number of pupils in grades in the village school in Mattoon. They had too many in his grade that year and not enough in the next grade, in which Ruth was enrolled. They decided to move some ahead.

The administrator of the school advanced a number of pupils who were considered the brightest; it was as simple as that. Ihno jokingly told me that if he was considered bright, there must have been some rather slow kids in his grade. Maybe Ihno was wrong about that.

Nonetheless, he did all right all the way though school "with Ruth's help at times," Ihno confessed to me recently. Ihno said that Ruth always paid attention better in school than he did. I guess her mind wasn't taken up with sports as much as his was. So he often got help from Ruth with his homework.

We, who were on the bottom side of the family, sometimes kidded Ruth, telling her that she and Ihno were just *experiments*—that *the folks weren't serious about a family* until they had five or six. She knew, of course, that we were joking, so she responded that she and Ihno thought the folks wanted only two; the rest were *afterthoughts*.

Ruth also retaliated to our kidding her by telling us, after all of us were growing up, that there were three parts to our large family—the *anticipated*, the *accepted*, and the *tolerated*.

If that was true, I was definitely in the *tolerated part*. Marcia and I were kind of the oldest of the youngest—she, of the four of us on the tail end, and I, as the oldest of *the three little boys* at the very end.

Actually, I have to say this for Ruth, it must have been difficult to be the oldest (especially *the oldest girl*) of so many children in the family. Think of it—*Ruth was eleven when I was born*, number seven! She was just seventeen, when the tenth was born.

Indeed, she must have seen me as *tolerated*. I'm sure there was no celebration led by Ruth when I came on the scene in 1928, only a few months after she turned eleven.

I think she already, by that time, had been groomed as an assistant "mother hen" to the rest of us and wasn't exactly thrilled about it.

When Danny, the tenth child in the family was born, Ruth and Ihno had just begun their senior year of high school! Dad and Mom decided to do something special at that time by choosing Ruth and Ihno to be *Daniel's godparents.*

How interesting! *The anticipated were asked not only to look after the youngest of the tolerated in the human sense, but were asked to look after him spiritually the rest of his life.*

So that Ruth and Ihno wouldn't be Dan's *only* godparents (maybe in case something happened *to them*), the folks invited Chip Menzel to join them. Chip (Clarence) was about Ruth's age. Brother Danny's birth and baptism were in 1934, just months before Ruth and Ihno graduated from high school in the spring of '35.

After Ruth and Ihno graduated, both of them naturally wanted to go to college. That wasn't a realistic wish at that time, however. The primary obligation of our parents was to feed and clothe *the multitude*, not to provide a college education for *the few*. They gave them the motivation to get more education, but they didn't have the resources to pay their way.

At that time, there weren't the scholarship opportunities like there are today. And our parents just couldn't afford to send them to college on what our father earned—about

$700 a year in 1935 (and the congregation wasn't always able *to pay that*).

I'm sure, however, that Mom and Dad were confident that Ihno and Ruth had a lot of potential. They probably grieved over not being able to send them on, though, like they would have liked to.

Probably, so that Ruth would at least go on with some education, they enrolled her in the Normal School for rural teacher students in Ortonville, seven miles from Odessa. In the meantime, Ihno was content to work for Kollitz's store in Odessa full-time to help pay the family's debt at that store.

I never heard either of them complain about not being able to attend a college or university right after high school. They knew there were good reasons, in a family the size of ours.

At first, Ihno stayed home so that Ruth could at least start her education. During the two years that Ihno worked in Odessa, there was no complaint on Ihno's part. Instead, he almost took the role of being a second father to us younger ones in the family.

When Ihno was at home, there was always fun for us. He even played softball with us during his noon hour from Kollitz's in the summer. And during a snowstorm or any bad weather, after household chores were done, Ihno organized word or song games that were so much fun that we prayed for the storm to continue.

During Christmas vacation, Ihno one time even planned an exciting tournament with putting together simple puzzles we had received as gifts at school. There were times too when Ihno helped us younger ones with our homework or with athletic skills.

When Ihno had time, he played basketball with us outside even in the cold of winter. Also, we played basketball in the large parsonage kitchen with a portable backboard and basket Ihno made that fit with ropes over the cellar door to hold it in place. Also, of course we used a small rubber ball.

Mother wasn't too happy with *our kitchen basketball games*, but she didn't say much; she knew we were having fun. Because Mom didn't like our playing basketball in the kitchen, though, we usually did the playing when she and Dad were gone to Yellow Bank on Sunday afternoons.

Ruth was already quite an accomplished pianist and church organist by the time she graduated from high school. However, she didn't complain about not being able to go on studying music at that time. She seemed content to attend the local teacher-training program. In the meantime, she often played for church services.

In the summer, Ruth helped Dad teach in the six-week summer school catechism sessions both at Trinity in Odessa and at the German Lutheran Church in Yellow Bank. She always took the youngest kids; she was especially good with the little ones.

Ihno was already quite a baseball player by the time he graduated from high school. There weren't opportunities at that time, however, to attend college on athletic scholarships such as there are today. Furthermore, Ihno wanted to study for the ministry. Baseball was a passion, but a secondary one. His greatest desire was to become a pastor.

Ihno finally enrolled at Concordia College in St. Paul to begin his ministerial studies in 1937. There, too, he played baseball and became an excellent pitcher.

Someone from the St. Paul Saints organization (International League) saw him pitch and invited him to practice with the Saints. (The Saints' ballpark was near Concordia College in St. Paul.)

He was invited to try out for the Saints, but he had his mind set on the ministry. He graduated from Concordia College in St. Paul in 1940 and from Concordia Seminary at St. Louis in 1945.

Sister Ruth taught in a one-room school north of Odessa for a year. *That was when a tradition was started in our family of financially helping each other.* Of the $40 a month that Ruth earned teaching in that one-room school, she sent $10 each month to Ihno at college.

She sent Ihno a part of what she earned, she said, because Ihno's working at Kollitiz's had helped her. She felt that Ihno's working to help the family made it more possible for her to attend the teacher-training program in Ortonville.

Most of the siblings in our family pretty much followed that tradition of helping others. That's how everyone who wanted it got a college education, and more than half of the brothers and sisters achieved a master's degree and more.

Of course, *no one in the family finished college in four consecutive years.* It wasn't that easy to work, study, and help each other. Some of us actually *took turns, studying and working.*

After teaching in the one-room school, Ruth entered the Lutheran School system and taught in a Christian Day School in the Montevideo, Minnesota, area. She also advanced her education wherever and however she could even after she got married.

After several years, she was asked to teach in a Lutheran school in Alexandria, Minnesota. While teaching there, she met Mark Richter, and the two were married in June of 1941.

I was not quite thirteen when Ruth and Mark were married, but I remember it well. We made up a story about how Ruth and Mark were both rather naive and somewhat shy. We said it happened when they were on their way from Odessa to Ortonville on their wedding night, where they planned to stay at the Columbia Hotel.

As we told the story, Mark's hand slipped off the gearshift in his '37 Ford coup on their way to Ortonville on their wedding night. The next thing, his hand was on Ruth's knee. Blushing, Ruth said, "We're married now, Mark. You can go farther, if you want to." So he drove all the way to Milbank, South Dakota.

Oh, well, it was just a story we liked to tell, but of course, it wasn't true. I still think it's funny.

Ruth was able to continue her education later, and she taught several years more and was a church organist in Green Bay, Wisconsin, where her husband, Mark, was an air traffic controller for the federal government FAA for a number of years.

Ruth and Ihno, the firstborns, certainly set the pace for the rest of us in the family. By helping each other, all of us were able to get much more education than our parents could afford.

The help-each-other tradition, started by Ruth and Ihno, also carried over to our parents later in life. Our father never had the benefit of a retirement program—not even Social Security. So at a family reunion in the mid-1950s, we siblings set up a program of our own for them.

We called it a *travel fund* so that it wouldn't seem like charity. Each of us contributed each month, and one of the brothers-in-law handled the funds and sent our parents a check each month. It helped them, I know. Dad still served a small parish, but the salary was meager.

Our dear parents had done so much for us by caring for us and bringing us up *to know and serve the Lord!* It was only right that we should do whatever we could to show them our gratitude in words and in deeds.

At this writing (2008), only four of us are still living of the ten born to our parents. However, of this I am confident: *We will all be together again! As Christ lives, we too shall live!*

We were all taught, "Sei getreu bis an den Tod, so wil ich dir die Krone des Lebens geben." ("Be faithful unto death, and I will give thee a crown of life" [Rev. 2:10].) We *believed it* here, and we will *know it* hereafter! As I said in the first chapter of this book, Dad had a plaque that said, "Serving the Lord doesn't pay much, but the retirement is out of this world."

I am writing this on April 9, 2008. On this very day, our father (born in 1888) would have been 120, and Ruth, the first born in our family, would have been 91. (She was Dad's birthday gift the day he turned 29, April 9, 1917.)

We will all be together again, after this life! Of that I am confident, and I know all my siblings were confident of that, also! *We have that confidence, not because of what we have done, but because of what our Savior, Jesus, has done for us!*

CHAPTER EIGHTEEN

POOL SPELLS "T-R-O-U-B-L-E"

Let everyone take his cue at the right time and in the proper place.

P-*o-o-l spelled trouble* in the musical *The Music Man*. That was just a story, but there was a day in my life when *pool really spelled trouble for me*—**BIG TROUBLE!**

Pool wouldn't have spelled trouble for every boy in the little town of Odessa, but I was a PK (preacher's kid). For me, the local pool hall was out of bounds—way out of bounds—in some parishioner's minds!

The people in Odessa didn't want to see the PKs at Barney's pool tables any more than they'd like to see their pastor father at Barney's bar guzzling a glass of Grain Belt draft!

Everybody in town knew everything about everybody. As I've previously said, "In Odessa, if you don't know what you're doing, call your neighbors. They'll know."

Back to the problem about pool: We younger boys in our family learned how to play pool on a small used table that had been given to us by our uncle Ted Thomaehlen, our mother's brother. Even with its warped bed and cracked balls, we had a lot of fun playing pool on that little table.

It was a lot more fun, though, to play on real pool tables like they had at Barney's in downtown Odessa. You couldn't bump those when you leaned against them, like we could the little pool table we had at home.

I didn't think it was wrong to play pool at Barney's; however, I knew Dad would have had something to say about it, and I was sure he wouldn't have liked the sign over the bar that read the following:

IF YOU DRIVE THE OLD MAN TO
DRINKIN', DRIVE HIM IN HERE!

I did nothing there but play pool, and I played only when there was no one in the place but a few of us boys.

Even then, I made sure there was someone nearby that I could give the cue to if one of Dad's parishioners would walk in. I was especially fearful that one of the officers of the church would show up while I was playing eight ball with the boys on a summer evening. A church officer would, I was sure, find a reason to come to the parsonage if he saw me there and talk about a "family problem"—a problem in *our family*, that is.

One day, I wasn't fast enough. While leaning over the table to make a shot, *one of the elders of the church* came in the door. And this was one of the *old German* elders who really took seriously his being an *assistant to the pastor.*

The man was a nice guy, but he sure was shaken to his rotund foundation when he saw me there.

"What do ya know, the preacher' kid's playing pool!" he growled when he came in the door and surveyed the joint.

I jumped! *I mean, I really jumped!* I tossed the cue to a friend, along with a nickel for my share of the game, and bolted out the back door like our cat springing away from a spark from our potbellied stove during a snowstorm!

Out in the alley, I kicked a can with my bare foot! I really wanted to kick myself on the part of my lower back where the Lord had split me! The tin can took its place since I couldn't quite reach back there.

"How could I get so careless?" I said to myself. "That guy will come down to the parsonage, for sure, to report to Dad what he saw. *I just know he will!"*

I knew I had to tell Dad myself before the elder would get there. But what should I say? What could I say that might keep holy smoke from rising from Dad's head?

I even thought of saying something like the confession of the prodigal son: *"Father, I have sinned against heaven and in they sight; I'm no longer worthy to be called thy son. Make me to be one of your servants."*

But that seemed a little *too canned.* Furthermore, my dad didn't have any servants. Something had to be said, though, and it had to be sincere!

When I got home, Dad was getting out of the car. I guess he'd been making hospital calls because he had his black suit on and was carrying a Bible.

Why did he have to look so much like a man of God when I had to face him with a pool hall problem? This could be worse than I thought at first—when I bolted out of the back door of Barney's!

I did finally face him, and I made a special effort to look and act humble. Nonetheless, I got a barrage of fire and brimstone like you couldn't imagine—in German, of course! He never could speak English when he was angry.

"Was werden die Leute sagen?" (What will the people say?) came out several times in that *deluge of gutteral syllables in the Kaiser's Deutsch!*

I got the usual sentence—an hour at attention in a straight-back chair in his study. I was hoping the elder who saw me at the pool hall had more than an hour of business to take care of in town. At least, I hoped it would take a little while before he'd come, so maybe I'd be "paroled" by that time.

He did come, though, just like I was sure he would! Fortunate for me, I'd finished my sentence by that time, so I ran upstairs into the bedroom above his study to listen through the register.

After *schwafling* (chatting) with Dad for ten minutes or so, he got to his real reason for coming to see the pastor.

"I gotta tell ya, Rever'n'," the rather large man began piously, "as much as I hate to do it " . . ." Boy, there was a whopper if you ever heard one, I thought. He'd come to our house *just to tell Dad* he'd seen me playing pool. Of that, I am sure. I was pretty sure he didn't really have any other reason to come.

Then he went on, "I saw one of yer sons at that *hellhole called Barney's* today. It was Arlo. He was playin' pool."

At first, Dad said nothing; he just listened intently. The man then sat back and said sanctimoniously, "He ran out pretty fast, when he saw me, but I know it was Arlo. He was shootin' pool with those ruffian kids who are in that *hellhole* all the time."

Dad put his elbows on his desk, as he asked slowly, "You did see him there?"

"Sure did, plain as day. Saw him when I came in the door."

"Well," Dad answered quite seriously, "Arlo has made his confession, and I've dealt with him."

Then, looking the man in the eye, he added, "So what was one of my Lutheran elders doing in that hellhole?"

CHAPTER NINETEEN

SUMMER EVENINGS IN ODESSA BEFORE TV

I'm writing this in January of 2008. A few days ago, while conversing with a teenage boy in a mechanic's shop, here where I live in Southeast Arizona, I mentioned that there was no television when I was a child. He said, "That must have been really boring!"

For the fun of it, I said, "Yeah, we just sat around most of the time, waiting for TV to come." He didn't know if he was supposed to laugh at that or not. Then I told him that I was just kidding.

There was indeed no TV in the '30s and '40s when I was growing up in Odessa, Minnesota, and to be sure, *we did not miss it!* For one thing, what you have never had, you don't miss. Also, there were always things to do.

We did have radio, of course, which I believe had many good programs, some of which we listened to. However, we didn't sit for hours with our ears fastened to the radio speaker like so many people sit with their eyes glued to the TV screen today.

I saw experimental TV while visiting Radio City Music Hall in New York City in 1946, the year I graduated from high school. It was interesting to see a telecast from one room to another, but I was not very impressed. In fact, in an English composition class in college that fall, I wrote a paper on how *impractical* I thought television would be, especially for sporting events.

The years have proved me wrong, of course, in some respects; although I can't to this day figure out why people pay good money to go to sporting events and sit in the highest part of the stadium when they can get *a better seat at home in their living room.*

But I can tell you that we, who were kids in the '30s and '40s, had a lot of fun in the evenings, and we went to bed *physically tired* from playing games, not *mentally exhausted* or disturbed from watching violent acts on TV or on video games.

As soon as school was out in the spring, there were games going on most evenings. Of course, most of us worked during the day mowing lawns (with push mowers), hoeing, and pulling weeds in our family gardens or helping at local businesses.

When we were little kids, we did a lot of running, playing *hide-and-seek, kick the can,* and a few rather clever games of that type. Sometimes we even played hide-and-seek-type games *on bicycles* over most of village. Talk about exercise! Our home base for "bike-hide-and-seek" was an unloading platform in the railroad yard across from the train depot near downtown.

Also, we frequently organized softball games, involving both boys and girls, especially if brother Ihno or our sister Adelheid were at home. Bud Holman was a pretty good organizer too. We usually played on *the square* on our church grounds.

Toward fall, it was football, which *we always played barefoot* to minimize injuries. We even *kicked* barefoot! (Believe it or not, some of us learned how to *drop-kick barefoot* without stubbing our toes. That's the way extra points after touchdowns were made at that time.)

When we were teenagers, we often played *run-sheep-run* and a couple of other more sophisticated games. At times, there were probably fifteen or more involved in those games—our family, the Holmans, the Calaises, the Wills, the Bumsteads, the Schultes, the Rodengens, the Gloeges, and a few others.

Also, after dark, we would sometimes build a campfire in the backyard of the parsonage where the whole gang would gather around for a marshmallow roast. We sometimes had a songfest too, especially if our sister Ruth was home to lead us in singing.

Also around the fire, we often told stories. In fact, at times, *we made up stories* with one starting and passing to another to continue and so on. Some kids were pretty creative, I must say.

There were *evening classes* too sometimes at the Odessa school. I remember one summer when the high school band teacher got some students to take lessons (instruments were furnished).

By the end of six weeks or so, we even had a ragtag "band." I know we didn't sound too great, but we were trying. I remember that one time we learned to play "Abide with Me," although our rendition may not have sounded too much like a sacred hymn.

"Abide with Me," with our limited ability, may have made the angels cover their ears, but I think they would have praised us for our efforts.

After the Jay Gould's carnival came to Odessa in 1938, we organized a "carnival" of our own. It wasn't much, and we didn't make any money at it, but we had a lot of fun, imitating some of the carnival games and acts. It took up many evenings; I know that.

We also had summer school at our church, taught by Dad and our older sisters, in the mornings for six weeks. A lot of kids attended. (There will be more on this in another chapter.)

One summer also, we set up a store. I think it was after the big fire in downtown Odessa when nearly a whole block of businesses burned to the ground. We maybe were thinking more about stores because of that. We set up the store in our woodshed, which was empty at that time. The shed had a large rolling door because it had been used as a garage. It was perfect for our use. It was almost as clean as a house after a bunch of us worked on it. Our sister Marty was the store manager.

We were given permission to use four or five backless church pews as shelves, which we stacked against one wall of the shed. The benches had been stored in the parsonage shed when they were not used for outdoor church activities.

After two or three weeks, we had most of those shelves stocked with cans and boxes. We got people to open their cans at the bottom and handle their cereal boxes, etc., with care, so they would still look real for our use though they were empty. We even stuffed bread wrappers to make them look real.

Cattails from a slough were our "wieners," and small painted chunks of concrete were made to look like "hamburgers." We also made up packages of flour, sugar, etc., in paper bags.

Quite a few adults came to see our store. After school started that fall, several teachers also came to visit the store. They were impressed with how we practiced business principles.

Leonard Kollitz even came to see our store. He was pleased to see that we had set things up more or less like at Kollitz's Fairway Fine Foods downtown Odessa. After he had seen our store, Mr. Kollitz gave us some cardboard store signs they were no longer using. Our store started to look pretty much like we were actually "in business."

One summer, a few of the teenage boys in town set up a boxing ring in the backyard across from Luenbergs' harness shop. I think the organizers, managers, and the boxers were Harris Semmler, Mike Calais, Arnie Nitz, and Bob Schulte.

They even charged a nickel or a dime when they staged bouts on Wednesday and Saturday nights while there were a lot of farm families in town.

The boys discouraged betting, though, because a couple of them had attended Dad's confirmation classes where gambling was given a *German Lutheran frown.*

If there was a breeze, late in the afternoon on summer days, we sometimes flew kites of all kinds, even some that were homemade. Bert Bohmert was the master kite flier. He showed us how to make kites and gave us suggestions about how to fly them, even when there wasn't that much wind.

One summer, Leroy (Babe) Anderson, as a part of his work in the government CCC program, took some of us boys on hikes to Sahr's Creek or the Minnesota River for marshmallow and wiener roasts. (We bought wieners two-for-a-nickel at Bohmert's Meat Market.) Also, Leroy taught us Boy Scout-type skills on those outings and sang patriotic songs with us.

No, there was no TV when we were kids in Odessa in the '30s and '40s, but there was never a lack of things to do. And although there were no angel teenagers in Odessa, I don't remember any of the kids getting involved with drugs or in trouble with the law.

Speaking of teenagers and trouble with the law, I guess you could say that things were pretty safe in Odessa at that time. I don't remember that we had a key for our house. Very likely, no one did. I wonder if even businesses were locked.

CHAPTER TWENTY

MISSIONFESTS IN ODESSA AND YELLOW BANK

In summer, each of the churches Dad served had what were called mission festivals. They were Sundays devoted entirely to missions. There were services both morning and afternoon usually with speakers from the mission field of the church, or at least visiting pastors who had at one time worked in missions. Of course, there were also offerings taken in the services for mission work.

The services were held outside, usually in the woods near the river. The Yellow Bank congregation had its own mission festival grounds in the woods along the Yellow Bank River not far from the church.

The Trinity congregation often used a place called DeWalds' Woods, just a few miles from Odessa, on the banks of the Minnesota River.

Some kind of a stage was set up as an altar. Often a large truck was brought in with a pump organ placed in the truck box, and a pulpit was set up in the back of the truck too.

There was no public address system, so the speakers had to be elevated a little higher than the audience and be of strong voice, so they could be heard. Some of the speakers, I remember, were bombastic enough to be heard by all, even by people who sat in their cars around the outside of the area set up as a sanctuary.

In DeWalds' Woods, where there was no permanent missionfest area, cement blocks were put on the ground, and planks borrowed from a lumberyard were placed on them to make benches for seating.

In Yellow Bank, where the church owned the wooded area on the river, permanent frameworks were in the ground for planks to be placed on them for benches. In both of those sanctuaries, there was seating for perhaps a hundred or more, and they were usually full for both the morning and afternoon services.

The mission festivals usually had a picnic atmosphere. At noon, between the services, there was always quite a dinner, more or less like a potluck. Everybody brought something. There was always plenty to eat for everybody.

Also, there was always a stand set up where ice cream and soda pop was sold. We, in our family, were ordinarily given each a nickel, enough for one ice cream cone or a bottle of pop.

One time I remember that Manny and I asked Dad for each another nickel. When he showed us his empty wallet, the mission speaker, who, I believe, was a missionary in

South America, dug in his pocket and gave each of us a nickel. We were thrilled and ran off to the stand for another purchase.

We boys usually wandered off in the Yellow Bank River area at the noon hour between the services, but we never went too far. We loved going to the bridge to throw stones into the murky water of the Yellow Bank River, which wasn't much more than a wide creek at the point.

Also, it was interesting to "investigate" the campground area nearby where the Methodists held retreats. They had wooden frameworks for tents, so I guess they stayed camped there for days at a time. They were never in session, though, when we had our mission festivals.

While looking around at the Methodist camp, I imagined what it would be like if we Lutherans stayed out in the woods there for several days. That sounded like fun! I thought it must be fun to be a Methodist, at least at their campout time.

Someone told me, though, that the Methodist sermons were pretty long at times, and they didn't even preach in German. In Yellow Bank, one of the services was always in German, which to a lot of Lutherans, seemed like a "holier" language.

I wondered sometimes if an old man in the Yellow Bank congregation wasn't right when he said that *the Lord spoke German*. The old man said that he was sure that the Lord spoke German because everywhere in scripture, when the Lord spoke, it said, "Und der Herr sprach " . . ." (And the Lord said . . .), and what the Lord said was always in German.

As a kid, I didn't quite understand how illogical that was. I just knew that German seemed like a holy language. Dad smiled when he heard the old German grandfather say that God spoke German, and our dad was even from Germany. Maybe Dad knew something about the Lord that we didn't know. I knew that prayers always sounded "more holy" in German. I thought maybe the Lord at least *preferred* German, especially when we spoke to Him.

Mission festivals were usually an enjoyable time for everybody. There was one time, though, at the mission festival in DeWaldses' Woods when it wasn't much fun. That was when some people from another religious group tried to upset the whole service one afternoon.

It was a group of people from a religious cult that was working hard at proselytizing in the Odessa area at that time. Several families who had been not very faithful Lutherans had become extremely devout members of that cult. They became, in fact, pretty fanatical, it seemed.

These cult members really wanted to let the world know (at least in the Odessa area) that they had found what they thought was *the truth!* They were of the opinion that mainstream Christianity was all wrong in its attitude toward the Bible. The cult people were especially *anti-Trinity.*

I was starting in confirmation class at that time, and I thought it was strange that they were so against the greatest mystery of the Christian Church taught in the Bible, the Holy Trinity! *Three in one—one in three;* who were we to question what God said about Himself in His holy Word?

We knew the word "trinity" was not used in the Bible, but we also knew that the idea of three-in-one and one-in-three certainly was taught in a number of ways in scripture.

Actually these cult members didn't have a church service or meeting of any kind there. They just came to where our service was held to try to upset things for us at our mission festival. There were only three or four men of the cult there, and they had their PA system set up on top of a car, aimed right at our group, across the river.

The Minnesota River, which had its source at Big Stone Lake just a few miles away, was a small stream in that area, so it was just a short distance across.

The men from the cult weren't even trying to hide or act like they were conducting a service of their own. They just felt, I guess, that they should give their message of *the truth, as they knew it,* to our people during our mission worship service. More than anything, it seems they wanted to disrupt the mission festival service.

As our people heard the blast of noise, I think they felt sorry for the people in the cult *who were known to them as former Lutherans who thought they had found the truth.* Our people were especially sorry that the cult members felt that this was the way to do things *to the glory of God.*

This was right *during the afternoon service.* As I said, we didn't have a public address system, nor would it have been good anyway for one group to try to drown out the other.

Our father, who was in charge of the missionfest, did the wise thing. He stopped the service, got the Lutheran elders together with him and the guest pastor, and tried to figure out what to do.

During the "noise break," many of the people went over to the stand to have another ice cream cone or a bottle of root beer as they waited to see what could be done.

Little more than a half hour went by, and the cult people on the other side of the river were still blasting away. Then all of a sudden, they stopped, packed up their gear, and left.

No one seemed to know quite what had happened, but since the noise interruption had vanished, Dad ordered our service to continue.

The rest of the day went as planned, and people went home that afternoon, wondering what had made the cult people with the loudspeaker change their minds.

Several days later, there was a little light shed on the subject. It seems that a teenager who worked at a produce shop in town remembered that there were about two dozens of bad eggs left in the garbage bin behind the shop the night before. That afternoon, he and a couple of other boys got an idea of how to *dispose of the eggs.*

They drove the three miles to town to get the eggs. When they returned, they lobbed them one at a time across the narrow river toward the menacing noise from the loudspeaker.

They said they didn't try to hit anyone; they just thought that the noise from the loudspeaker and a *hydrogen sulfide smell from the "overripe" eggs* would not mix too well.

The interesting thing about this was that, although a lot of people found out what happened, our Dad was never told. If he had found out, I don't think he'd have been at all pleased. I don't know, however, what he would have done. As far as I know, he never even tried to find out what happened.

Mission festivals were usually quite enjoyable. Even the day the cult people tried to interrupt things, it turned out all right.

Arlo age 4

Seven J. siblings in 1932. Ihno made the truck.

Arlo age 14

The Janssen family, December 1942.

Arlo, Manny, Dad, Danny,
and Marty in the backyard, 1937.

Ihno and our new '36 Chevrolet.

Immanuel Church, Yellow Bank.

Drawing of Trinity Church and parsonage.

Janssens with Thormaehlen relatives,
Arlo in Dad's arms, 1929.

Thormaehlen family on Mom and Dad's
wedding day, July 5, 1916.

Danny and Manny, fall of 1943.

Arlo and Manny with some of our ducks, 1938.

Downtown Odessa after the snowstorm of 1940.

Five youngest siblings with Mom and Dad, 1944.

Odessa Elementary Rhythm Band.
Lower right, Arlo, 1935.

Five youngest siblings with Mom and Dad, 1943.

A letter from one of the kids.

Last time nine siblings were together,
Minnesota, 1985.

Arlo and Manny, off to do farmwork, 1942.

"Three little boys" with a day's catch, 1940.

The house Dad built for Stromers in 1910.

Arlo at fourteen, 1942.

Cotton Blossom Singer's "House Bus."

Mom, Dad, and Arlo—the day Arlo left
for prep school. September, 1944

Odessa School District 24, 1947.

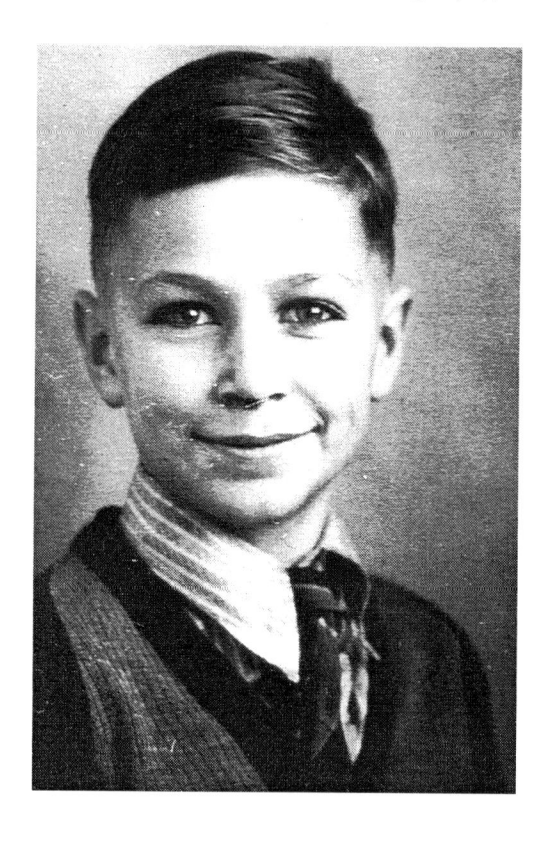

Cat-that-ate-the canary look, 1939.

Mom and Dad in parsonage yard, 1944.

Part of Janssen reunion group, 1946.

Four pastors: Ihno Senior and three sons, 1959.

Vernon, Nita, Marty, Mom, Manny, and Arlo.

Last reunion with both parents,
Merrill, Wisconsin, 1959.

Arlo and wife,
Ofelia—year of their marriage in 1972).

St. Martin's Day School, Shawano, Wisconsin.

Arlo, the College teacher in 1966.

Arlo, Manny, Danny, and Ihno in Odessa, 1976.

Arlo, Marcia, Vernon, Adelheid, and Anita, 1933.

CHAPTER TWENTY-ONE

PLAY OF CHILDREN IN ODESSA IN THE '30s AND '40s

No, we didn't have television, and we didn't listen to the radio very much, but it seems there was always something to do when we were children.

In our own family, we were enough children near the same age to have fun together, and there were children our age also in the neighborhood.

In the winter, after school and on weekends, when we weren't busy with homework or household chores, we often were out on the hill with sleds, or we were playing games in the snow.

We even played basketball outside in the winter. Maybe we didn't play as well with jackets and overshoes or boots on, but we did play basketball in our backyard. After all, the basketball season is in winter, isn't it? The basket was on a backboard on the side of the barn, and the "court" was usually packed-down snow.

No matter how cold it was, we played basketball outside *for hours*. Sometimes the only time we went indoors was to warm up the ball. In the cold weather, the ball would lose its bounce, so we'd go and "revive it" in the house.

A teacher explained to us what happened to the air in the ball, but we just knew that when it was cold, the ball wanted to go inside to warm up every once in a while.

It was okay, because we usually need to warm up too.

Thinking of winter, we always had a lot of chores to do, especially chopping wood and bringing wood, coal, and kindling into the house for our stoves. And very frequently there was snow to shovel—plenty of it at times.

Of course, we did a lot of playing indoors too. We didn't have as many toys as some children had, but we made do with what we had. We got pretty fancy at times with the tinker toys and erector set, even though both sets had been given to us used and not quite all the pieces were there. That didn't make a lot of difference; we improvised.

We also had a lot of fun with puzzles. Those, too, were given to us, and some pieces were missing. We had some puzzles with as many as a thousand pieces or more.

Big brother Ihno taught us how to have fun even with smaller fifty-piece puzzles that we had received as gifts at school. He helped us organize tournaments. We put all the pieces of each puzzle facedown, and then two of us would race, turning the pieces over and trying to put the puzzle together the fastest.

Sometimes we raced putting the puzzles together with the pictures *upside down or sideways*. It was fun, especially with a number of us competing together. At times even the older ones in the family participated with us. That was more fun. That was more often during Christmas vacation when more of the family was home together.

When the older ones in the family were home during the holidays, some evenings we played *Rook*, our favorite card game.

Dad and Mom even joined in the *Rook* game sometimes. Dad was a lot of fun when he played cards with us, especially when he won the bid. He always made it sound like he was playing scientifically, but it didn't always work that well for him and those he took along in the bid.

It was humorous having Mom in the Rook game. When she looked through her bifocals to see her cards, she held them out so far that everyone else could see them too. Then, too, Mom and the girls would often jabber while we were playing; that made passing cards from one to another in *jokingly cheating* so easy, it wasn't even a challenge. Dad sometimes would tell us, "Don't cheat unless you can cheat fair." He knew we were just kidding, but he still didn't care much for it.

We kids also played Monopoly, which was always a lot of fun. We modified the rules of the game, which I think added enjoyment to the game. For one thing, we allowed players to borrow from the bank. Figuring out interest added to the skill of the game. Also, we placed the money from fees and penalties on the FREE PARKING corner and gave the money to anyone who landed there. When there was a bad snowstorm in the winter, we sometimes continued a Monopoly game for several days, only taking time off to eat, do our chores, or work on homework.

Thinking of snowstorms reminds me of what happened at times early in the morning. If we woke up to hear a howling wind, and we'd hear the phone ring, it was usually someone calling to say there would be no school. That was reason to cheer.

We got up faster on those mornings than we did when we had to go to school. The first thing we would do was to get enough wood and coal in, take care of any other chores, and then get a game of Monopoly or some other game going.

A snowstorm was always a serious matter for many people, but for us kids it was a lot of fun. I'm sure our parents weren't that happy to have us home all day, but it surely was an enjoyable time for us. We never lacked something to do.

Brother Danny, the youngest in the family, told me in recent years that he sometimes prayed for the snowstorm to continue because we had so much fun playing games. Maybe he did pray like that. Whether his prayers were answered or not, I do not know. All I know is that storms did sometimes continue for days, and we had *tons of fun* those stormy days after our work was done.

Summer too was a fun time for us kids. We always had something to do. When we were little kids, we loved playing with little cars and building roads in the sandbox and in the dirt under the trees between the parsonage and the church. Sometimes we built elaborate "towns" and "farms" under the trees. Our toys weren't the greatest, but it didn't matter; we had fun with the things we had.

Also, we rolled old tires, playing like they were our vehicles. When we had larger truck tires, we went up the hill by the Drefeens. Then one of us would get in the middle of the tire, and others would get it started to roll down the hill. We got dizzy enough from rolling down the hill, but it was worse when the tire, rolling "sixty per," would hit a tree or roll into a deep ditch.

We did have an old wagon that Ihno bought at a farm auction for a dollar and fixed up for us. We used it to play or work in the garden or the yard. If we had weeds or grass to haul, we'd play *horse and wagon,* two pulling and one *driving the team.*

Of course, there was work to be done in the garden that couldn't always be done as fun—like pulling weeds and hoeing the potato rows. We tried, though, to make anything fun, if possible. Sometimes we'd race to see who could hoe a row of potatoes the fastest.

The work always went faster that way and was a little more enjoyable. Of course, the work was always subject to inspection by Dad, but he wasn't too adversely critical most of the time.

Marcia loved roller skating. The skates we had, usually some that were given to us, weren't the greatest, but that didn't keep us from having fun. The sidewalks weren't so wonderful either, so we looked around the neighborhood for sidewalks that were better.

Ed Menzel and George Gloege both had sidewalks that were smoother than most in the neighborhood. I'm sure we made a lot of noise skating near or around their houses, but they didn't complain. They probably said, like Dad did when we made noise playing around our house, "Lasz ihn doch gehen." (Let them go.)

We also played with what we called a "hoop and wheel." Why we called it that, I don't know because "hoop" and "wheel" sound more or less like the same thing. What it was, though, was a steel wheel like a ring about ten inches in diameter, which we pushed around with a piece of lath with a short piece across the bottom of the stick forming a T.

It doesn't sound like much, but it was a lot of fun. We sometimes even decorated the lath stick with whatever paint we could find. Pushing these wheels around too was like we were operating vehicles; at least that's how we thought of them when we were playing. Usually we even made a sound like a car as we ran around with them. Cars at that time made rather distinctive sounds.

After the six weeks of summer school was over (toward the end of July), we frequently went swimming or fishing in the Minnesota River. The bullheads were the easiest to catch in the early morning. They were a little hard to handle because they had sharp spikes on their heads, but we learned fairly well how to handle them without getting bloody.

Mom was ordinarily in favor of our going fishing because we brought home enough fish for dinner. And she liked it that we also did the cleaning of the fish. I do remember one time, though, when we went fishing, and we didn't have permission. That time we didn't catch anything till we got home, if you know what I mean.

The hot Minnesota summer afternoons were the best time to go swimming. The Minnesota River wasn't the greatest for swimming, especially in the middle of the summer when the water was low and a little murky. However, we had a special swimming hole on a bend of the river, just down the back side of the school hill. The water was a little deeper there.

What I've written in this chapter is mainly about our playing *when we were smaller children*. There's more about things we did when we were a little older in the chapter about *summer evenings*.

No, we didn't have TV when we were children, but we didn't miss what we had never had. Also, it seems we always had something to do, though, and we didn't feel deprived; I know that.

It is my hope that children, especially in small towns like Odessa, put down their video games, take their eyes away from the TV, and still frequently get outside to have fun something like we did those many years ago.

CHAPTER TWENTY-TWO

AS A KID, I LEARNED ABOUT GAMBLING!

As I have said, I became a paperboy when I was about thirteen. Quite often the last delivery I made on my paper route was at Barney's pool hall downtown in little Odessa. I didn't have to go there last, but I preferred to do it that way.

The pool hall was usually empty at that time, about six in the evening, so I could relax at the end of my route with a bottle of pop. Or if there was another kid there, I could sometimes even shoot a game of pool with little or no fear of being seen by any of my father's parishioners at that time of day.

One day in November of 1941 (I was thirteen), I stopped at the pool hall to collect for the paper. There was no one in the place except Barney Hill, the proprietor. I ordered a bottle of Pepsi and waited for Barney to pay me for the paper.

Barney was playing the nickel pinball machine and had just won about forty cents when I walked in. He paid me the twenty-three cents for the paper, partly with the money he had just won.

After he paid me for the paper, Barney put down another nickel and said, "I'll give you this, kid, but I'd like to see you put it in the pinball machine."

I had never played the pinball machine. I knew that some of my friends called it "the nickel eater," so I had always stayed away from it.

Then, of course, there was Dad to think about. If he had known at that moment *that I was even thinking about it,* his feathers would be ruffled enough that his tongue would switch gears from English to German, and his penetrating eyes would glare.

I also knew that the first thing Dad would say was, "Vas werden die Leute sagen?" (What will the people say?) I had heard that question often enough in my life that it rang in my head every time I was tempted to do anything the least bit questionable.

I said to Barney, "I better not play the pinball machine. I'd get a German sermon delivered just to me if my dad knew I was even talking to you about it."

"Hey," Barney responded, "the nickel's not even yours yet. I just put it down here and said I'd like to see you put it in the machine."

Well, I thought, what could be the harm? It's really still Barney's, I reasoned. Also, I had watched some guys play it, and I sometimes wondered what it was like to play the machine myself.

I looked toward the door! No one was coming, so I quickly put the nickel in the slot and pulled the spring shooter. Without even using the flippers or bumping the machine, I won two nickels.

As the nickels dropped into the drawer below, I should have been happy, but I felt nervous! Very nervous! My hands were shaking, and I felt sweaty. Somehow, this didn't seem right.

"Wow! Look at that. You won without trying." Barney laughed, "You better put at least one of those back in there to show your appreciation."

No one was still around, so I did it; I put in one of the nickels I'd just won. I pulled the spring shooter and stepped back. Lights flashed, and one light stayed on—the one that said, "SWEEPSTAKES!"

When I saw the lights flash, my heart almost thumped out of my chest! Barney jumped when he saw the Sweepstakes light on. "I don't believe it!" Barney blurted out. "That light hasn't come on in over two weeks!"

Then, kind of quietly, he said with a sly smirk on his face, "Did I see ya foldin' yer hands when ya put that nickel in?"

I was really nervous—so nervous, I couldn't stand still. "Honest, I'm not trying to involve the Lord in this," I said, *shaking in my boots*. "Fact is, this could be the devil's doing!" Sweating, I asked Barney, "What do I do now?"

"Well, kid, you ain't won it yet, but you got a chance!" Then he pointed to another light that came on. "Look! It says *$50!* You gotta a chance to win *fifty smackaroos!*"

I backed away and looked again toward the door because I was afraid somebody would come in that I didn't want to see me there, especially playing the nickel eater.

Barney stepped up close to me. "What ya gotta do now, kid," he said as calmly as he could, using gestures, "is shoot the ball and coax it to go all the way down to the *scratch slot* at the bottom of the board. You can use the flippers, ya know, and nudge the machine, but don't do it too hard. If the tilt light comes on, it's all over."

He stood beside the machine and said with a broad smile, "If ya make it, your fifty bucks will be comin' to ya!" Then, with a smile, he added, "I bet you'd like that. Wouldn't it be nice, so close to Christmas 'n' all?"

I was literally quivering; I even had tears in my eyes, I was so nervous! My head even hurt. "One problem!" I said, almost crying, my voice shaking. "I couldn't go home with fifty dollars! No, sir! My dad would make me bring it back!"

Just then, a businessman from Ortonville walked in, who lived near Odessa and often stopped in for a beer and a game of pool on his way home.

He saw Barney and me and noticed how nervous I was, so he asked what was going on. Barney, who knew the man well, told him.

Barney also told him that I was a preacher's kid and that I'd said I couldn't go home with fifty dollars. The man stepped close to me and said with his hand over his mouth and a smile on his face, "Well, kid, could you go home with two bucks?"

I looked a bit puzzled, not just because of his question, but because two kids I knew walked in just then and heard the conversation.

They were nice guys, but I knew they didn't usually keep things to themselves. *Now this whole thing would be all over town; I just knew it!* That made me more nervous.

"I'll give you two bucks, if you let me shoot the ball," said the man. "What do you say?"

He held out two dollars, and I reluctantly took it. One of the boys said, "You just lost yourself forty-eight bucks!"

When the other kid saw the flashing light with the amount of the sweepstakes, he exclaimed, with his eyes wide open, "Fifty bucks! Wow! Betcha my dad doesn't make that in a month, cuttin' hair!"

Barney, however, said I did the wise thing. "You've got two bucks in your hand, and, like ya said, you can go home with that much," he said encouragingly, patting me on the shoulder. "He's still got to do his part. Let's see if he can do it."

The man obviously was an experienced pinball player. He pulled the spring-shooter gingerly, worked the flippers, and bumped the machine like he really knew what he was doing.

The ball bounced around like a drunken bum, but in spite of the man's encouragement, it fell into a number hole just before the scratch slot.

The man hit the machine with his fist and said a few things I never heard at our house, except in a theological sense. Then he backed away, spewed out a couple more colorful words, and ordered a Grain Belt draft.

I offered the man his two dollars back, though one of the boys said I was stupid to do that. The man, however, wouldn't take the two dollars. "No, kid, keep it," he said, slapping the wooden bar. "A deal's a deal. This just ain't my day." Then he chugalugged his glass of beer.

I was sure this whole thing would be spread all over town. Having those two boys know what happened was like printing it in the *Ortonville Independent!*

I said nothing that night at home to anybody. The next day, I bought my brother and sister, Manny and Marty, each a nickel ice cream cone at Bellnap's. Then I told them how I happened to have the two dollars and pleaded with them not to tell the folks. Then, I added, "And for sure, don't say anything to little brother Danny!"

Manny laughed when I mentioned Danny. "Well," I said, "you know very well how *he shares all secrets with Dad.*" Then he and Marty really laughed; they knew what I was talking about!

The next Sunday, I put a quarter in the Sunday school collection, a little more than a tithe, I figured, on the two dollars.

I didn't know if the Lord let me off with that, or if He was just merciful toward a bungling PK who did some pretty stupid things sometimes. This sure was one of them.

Miraculously, the whole thing blew over, without Dad finding out. I had to thank Manny and Marcia for keeping their traps shut! I was also happy that those two boys that came into the pool hall when that happened weren't on a neighborly chat-over-the-fence basis with Dad. If they had been, I'd have been in trouble—big trouble!

To this day, about three score and seven years later, I don't put a nickel (or anything) in gambling machines, I don't go to casinos, and I don't play the lottery! I learned my lesson, and I can truthfully say, "I'm about two dollars ahead in the gambling business."

CHAPTER TWENTY-THREE

HALLOWEEN IN ODESSA, AWHILE AGO!

Is it really a hallowed evening before
All Saints Day?

When I lived in the city of Philadelphia, Pennsylvania, in the 1950s, Halloween was fun for most children. Some children, in fact, didn't know the meaning of "trick" in the expression "trick or treat."

On Halloween evening at that time, a neighbor boy of about six and his sister came to our door saying, "Trick or treat." For the fun of it, I asked the boy what kind of trick he had in mind. He answered happily, "I can do a *somersault.*" And with that he showed me on the grass in front of the house.

There was no trick or treat activity on Halloween while I was growing up in the village of Odessa, Minnesota, in the '30s and '40s. It was all trick—no treat—at that time! And to be sure, there was no thought on the part of teenage boys to do somersaults on your lawn. What some boys did to the townspeople in Odessa were things they claimed *the devil made them do*. And I think they were right.

Teenage boys thought they were having fun, but there wasn't any enjoyment for the people who were the butt of their jokes and pranks. No doubt the devil had something to do with their actions, but I think they could have resisted his temptation without much trouble.

I realize that through the years, Halloween has become fun for kids in most parts of the country, and stores make a lot of money because of it. That still doesn't make it right.

I've never liked Halloween. It is anything but *a* "hallowed evening" before All Saints Day, and what I remember about it in Odessa when I was growing up was that it only caused problems, sometimes big problems!

The favorite activity of some teenage boys in the '30s and '40s in Odessa was *tipping outhouses*—toilets that were small separate buildings. They had a *field day* with that activity because almost every home in town and nearby farms had a *three-holer* on the property. Almost no houses in that area had bathrooms at that time.

Of course, there were people who tried to protect their *backyard comfort huts*. One man, I remember hearing about, sat on his back porch all night long with a loaded shotgun. One shot in the air when boys came near scared *the devil's helpers* away. I guess that worked for him.

Another man, I was told of, sat *in his privy* with a loaded shotgun, thinking he'd come out when he'd hear the boys come near and scare the *you-know-what* out of them. The problem was that boys found out he was inside the outhouse, so they sneaked up and tipped the little building over *onto the door*. I'm not sure how the guy got out of his *facedown three-holer* with the door facing in the wrong direction.

Sometimes the tide was turned. For example, when a man found out that Halloween night was going to be *moonless,* he and his sons *moved their outhouse* over a few feet.

In the darkness, a few boys showed up to tip the privy, and would you believe, one of them fell into the "sweet violets." Think of it, friends, *there was not a garden hose in our town, nor was there a place to take a shower in all Odessa!* Not at that kid's house! Not at any house! I think he spent the rest of the night giving the fish in the Minnesota River a basic *nature* whiff *of Odessa* by washing his *birthday suit* and rinsing out his store-bought clothes in the river current.

Another ingenious man *lay in wait with his two sons* on their farm near Odessa. The youthful *assistants of Satan* didn't bother the outhouse, but they took apart an old horse buggy and carefully reassembled it on top of the farmer's hog barn.

The farmer and his sons watched them for hours from behind some bushes. When the pranksters had completed *their masterpiece* a little before dawn, the farmer and his sons came out with their shotguns loaded with birdshot and said, "Nice job, boys. Now, let's see you take it down."

Those mechanical geniuses must have worked *till the cows came home* to undo their work of art. What poetic justice!

There was another example of poetic justice I heard of at a one-room school north of Odessa. Boys perched a pan of water over a door in the school, in hopes that the young teacher would *have her hairdo drenched* when she would push the door.

However, one of the boys who was a pupil in that school wanted to see the teacher get doused, so he offered to carry her books into the school the next morning. The problem was that he made a mistake while helping the teacher and bumped the door himself. *Guess who got doused!*

Incidentally, no one from our parsonage family was allowed out on Halloween night. Our parents were very strict about that! Even brother Vernon who often claimed that *the devil made him do a few things* was kept in.

Only our pastor father went out on Halloween night—*to patrol the streets*! Dad was more of a deterrent than the one-eyed town marshal in the village. Dad knew all the boys in town, and they all knew him—and *feared seeing him* when they were involved in monkey business.

When they saw Dad on Halloween night, they'd usually say, "We're on our way home, Reverend! Honest we are!" And to which Dad would answer, "Then, go! Now! And get out your Bibles and check to see how to show love for your neighbor!"

When I discussed what I was writing about Halloween in Odessa with an old friend who still lives in that area of Minnesota, he told me something I didn't know: in the days when A. E. Pagel was the principal of the Odessa school, he told the boys that were trying out for basketball the day after Halloween that if they didn't put back up all the outhouses in the village they had laid flat, they would be considered ineligible for the team that season.

When the boys heard that, they may have said the expression "sweet violets!" and several synonyms for the expression, but Mr. Pagel was not a man to be messed with.

Needless to say, the *outdoor comfort stations* they had tipped Halloween night were uprighted in broad daylight, and some apologies were made to the householders. *Those guys wanted to play basketball!*

Incidentally, our *parsonage three-holer* was built into an outbuilding behind the parsonage, which also housed a woodshed, workshop, chicken coop, and garage. *There was no way our outhouse could be laid flat to the ground.*

Undoubtedly, that parsonage outhouse was designed by Halloween-conscious church trustees. They made it truly German Lutheran—*steadfast and immovable.*

Also, the church outhouse attached to a woodshed between the church and the little church school was just as German-Lutheran-sturdy. It would have taken Paul Bunyan's help to tip that one over!

To this day (I'm writing this in 2007), I don't care for Halloween. I remember that it caused "devil made me do it" problems in our little town years ago.

I also remember how the favorite Halloween activity of teenage boys in Odessa in the '30s and '40s made it difficult for some people *to answer the call of nature the morning after*, on All Saints Day.

CHAPTER TWENTY-FOUR

FIRST, WE WASHED OFF AT THE RIVER

In the summer of 1942, when I was thirteen and brother Manny eleven, we got a job shoveling coal at Menzels' Lumber and Coal Yard in Odessa.

The job was to empty a freight boxcar of forty tons of coal, transporting it across a causeway of boards from the railroad car into the bins in the coal sheds. We had two days (forty-eight hours) to unload each boxcar.

The pay was twenty-five cents a ton. That figured to ten dollars for a forty-ton carload. Over a period of six weeks, we did ten of those carloads, taking two days of eight to ten hours for each carload.

What we did with most of the $100 we earned made Manny and me feel pretty good because we felt that we were helping the family. I'll say more about that a little later.

The equipment we had to work with the coal was a wheelbarrow, two shovels, and our young bodies, such as they were at that time.

When Junior Mews saw me there one day without a shirt on, he said I could have helped a biology class cheat by raising my shirt and letting them count my ribs. Nice guy.

Manny and I usually went barefoot in the summer, but Dad made us wear some old well-worn tennis shoes while we worked there in the coal yard. He was afraid we'd cut our feet on the pieces of coal if we were barefoot.

There was an awful lot of dust, but we didn't wear anything on our noses and mouths. We tried one day wearing a wet hankie over our mouths, but it just seemed too hard to breath that way. We didn't wear gloves either because our hands were pretty tough from doing other kinds of work.

We were so full of coal dust when we came home for lunch that sister Marcia brought us something to eat out under the trees between the parsonage and the church.

We knew that sister Marcia didn't think we ought to go inside the house while we were so full of coal dust, but she was nice about it. She made it seem as though we were having a picnic out on the lawn under the trees. Marty always ate something with us too, and so did little brother Danny.

After lunch, we'd sprawl out on the grass for a short siesta. Little brother Danny kept flies away from our dusty, sweaty bodies while we rested. That way he felt he was a part of our project. He was only seven years old.

When we came home at the end of each day, Mom sent us to the river to first wash off as much dust as we could. Then she scrubbed us outside of the house by the backyard pump before we could go into the house. She wasn't too gentle with her scrubbing, and she used homemade soap, which really burned in our eyes.

What made us feel good was that, as Mom scrubbed us, she praised us for helping the family. She knew what we intended to do, but we hadn't told Dad yet.

After several weeks, when we got the first forty dollars, we gave thirty-five of it to Dad for a month's payment on our 1936 Chevy. The new car cost $850. The men in the congregation had said they would help Dad pay for the car, but they couldn't help much.

Fred Schueneman had given Dad a loan so he could pay off the dealer in Ortonville who had warned that the car could be repossessed. It was good of Mr. Schueneman to lend Dad the money, but that summer Dad had a hard time paying Fred too.

When we gave Dad the $35 for the July payment to Fred Schueneman, he was so choked up that he almost couldn't talk. After he got his voice back, he told us to take the money to Mr. Schueneman ourselves and tell him how we earned it.

We went over to Schueneman's house that evening and told him how we had earned the money for this payment. It kind of shook up Fred too. Manny said when we were going home that it was interesting to see an old bachelor like Fred Schueneman have tears in his eyes.

Manny and I didn't think we were doing such a great deed. After all, the car was the family's. Also, brother Ihno had done much more for the family when he worked at Kollitz's store full-time for two years to help pay our large family's debt at the store and make it possible for sister Ruth to start teacher training.

When we took Mr. Schueneman the August payment, he sent his sister out to meet us, when he saw us coming. That kind of amused us but made us feel good too, in a way, to think of what they thought of our helping the family this way.

The only thing that bothered us about the job that summer was that we found out that a man, *doing the same thing* at the coal yard, was earning *fifty cents* a ton—$20 a carload. And he took just as long as we did to get the boxcars emptied.

Yes, that was *a ton*; we were not working *by the hour*. When we got up enough courage to ask the man who hired us, he said simply, "Do you want to work, or don't you?"

We wanted to work, so we said no more. I think, however, we would have joined the Kids' Coal Workers' Union that day, if there had been such an organization.

Of course, it probably wasn't even legal for him to hire young kids, and we were glad to help the family.

By the way, with our help that summer and a few more pitch-ins from others in the family, *we got our '36 Chevy paid for by the end of 1942!*

CHAPTER TWENTY-FIVE

A FOURTH OF JULY WHEN FUN TURNED TO TRAGEDY FOR A BROTHER WHO NEVER LOST HIS SPIRIT!

When the Fourth of July fell on a *Sunday*, usually Trinity Church in Odessa had a picnic on the church grounds. A time I especially remember when that occurred was 1943.

The day was fun for everyone until tragedy struck in the middle of the afternoon.

After church and Sunday school in the morning, there was a big outdoor barbeque and potluck dinner set up under the trees between the parsonage and the church. There was enough food for an army, and there was a wonderful variety. All the people had as much as they desired.

After everyone rested a bit and chatted with friends, they gathered *on the square* next to the church school, and the games were started. First came the activities for the youngest children, then for the older kids, and finally some humorous games for the adults—those folks who were brave and physically fit enough to participate.

Mr. Pagel, the superintendent of the Odessa school, set up a speaker with music for the picnic area. Later, he arranged to have it projected to the area where the games were held. Everyone was having a wonderful time, and the weather was perfect. It didn't seem like a black cloud could change the day for everybody in an instant.

After the games for various groups, a softball game was organized with the married men competing with *the singles*—"Those who as yet had not made the same mistake once," as one of the old men quipped. The game too was on *the church square.*

Ihno, who was there that weekend with his girlfriend, Shirley Till, organized the game and pitched for the single men's team. He suggested some special rules to accommodate the older men who were not too physically spry anymore. Everyone agreed, and the game got under way.

The game was great fun for all—those who played on the two teams and the many people watching and cheering-on the players.

In the fifth inning, the score was tied at five. (Of course, the married men had been *spotted* three runs.) One of the single boys, a strong farmer's son, took a *baseball bat* in hand, although this was a softball game, and stepped up to the plate. There he stood and swung the bat in the air a few times, just to get the feel of it.

The young man was a good hitter; they all knew that. Someone challenged this big strappin' farm boy to hit it over the trees in left field, so he was really aiming to clobber the ball.

Brother Manny, who was twelve years old, was sitting next to Dad behind the third-base line, next to Schuett's garden fence. After the batter hit two long foul balls, for some reason, Dad got up, and Shirley Till sat in his place next to Manny. They chatted together a little, then cheered the teams on.

With two strikes on him, the young man with the baseball bat in his hands was still determined to clobber the ball over the trees. As the ball came right where he wanted it, he swung with all his might. To everyone's surprise, he missed the ball entirely *and let go of the bat! The heavy-ended baseball bat went flying!*

In an instant, the bat whirled through the air, the handle slamming against Shirley's shoulder, snapping the large end of the bat right into brother Manny's mouth with tremendous force!

Manny crouched and fell forward to the ground, not making a sound! People nearby thought he was dead! When they rolled him over, he was in a pool of blood; *still there was no sound from him!*

Mr. Pagel hurriedly knelt over Manny! He found that he was still breathing, and his heart was beating, but Manny had been seriously injured and was bleeding profusely.

Herman Pansch knelt down to assist Mr. Pagel. By this time, almost everyone at the picnic was gathered around. Our mother who had been sitting near Manny was almost hysterical. Women were trying to calm her down.

Mr. Pagel, with Herman's help, got Manny into Pansch's car. Then, with Dad holding Manny in the backseat with towels held to his face, they rushed to the hospital in Ortonville, seven miles away.

Dr. Bolsta, who had been called as they left, met them at the hospital. An oral surgeon was also called in to help the doctor. They found that Manny had a broken jaw and was missing four or five teeth. They couldn't determine how many teeth were actually missing because his jaw was so badly injured and swollen.

They stitched him up the best they could. It was difficult because there was a tremendous amount of swelling in the entire lower part of the head, including, of course, the jaw.

Manny was kept in the hospital, and Dad stayed with him. Also, Mother was brought up there later that night and stayed with him too.

The next morning, when we were told by phone that Manny had lost some teeth, sister Marcia and I looked to see if we could find the teeth on the ground where he had fallen. The doctors were interested in finding out, if possible, how many teeth had been knocked out.

When we told the doctors that we were not able to find as much as one tooth, he said that Manny had probably swallowed them.

It was a blessing that the bat did not strike Manny *just inches higher* on his face, or he very likely could have been killed or had brain damage that would have made the tragedy even greater.

Months later, Manny had more surgery and a bridge put into his mouth. I don't know how many surgeries and different medical procedures were performed in his mouth, both in Minnesota and later in Wisconsin in the following years.

We were all grateful to God for Manny's progress through the years. However, that very serious injury, which ended the men's ball game at that Fourth of July picnic in 1943 and changed the fun to tragedy that day, plagued Manny for the rest of his life.

Nonetheless, even with a bridge in the front of his mouth which constantly caused him problems, Manny not only studied for the ministry, but graduated with honor, was ordained into the ministry, and served parishes in Texas, Illinois, and California.

In addition to that, for a number of years before his untimely death in 1989, Manny was the personal assistant to the president of Concordia Seminary in St. Louis and later also to the president of the Lutheran Church—Missouri Synod.

Although Manny was so seriously injured when a black cloud hung over the 1943 church picnic, he never lost his spirit or his sense of humor. One classic example of his humor is the following:

> *When Manny was traveling extensively in one of his synodical positions, he arrived one day at a Cleveland, Ohio, airport hotel to find that they did not have his reservation, and*

the hotel was totally booked. This happened, I believe, in 1984 or '85. I know it was while Ronald Reagan was our president.

Manny told the hotel personnel that he had meetings scheduled with church leaders at their hotel all the next day, so it was very important that he stay there. "Sorry," they said. "We don't have your reservation, and the hotel is filled. There's nothing we can do."

Manny sat and thought for a moment, then returned to the registration desk and said, "If President Reagan were to show up here today, would you find him a room?"

The answer was, "I suppose so. Why are you asking?" Manny nonchalantly answered, "He's not coming, I'll take the room."

Believe it or not, *they appreciated his humor enough to review his case, and they finally found a room for him!* The next day, his meetings went on as planned.

Another example of Immanuel's humor: For a number of years, he worked in stewardship and financial development. That was at the time when some Christians were using a bumper sticker that said, "HONK, IF YOU LOVE JESUS!" Manny suggested that the bumper sticker rather read, "TITHE, IF YOU LOVE JESUS! ANY GOOSE CAN HONK!"

Naturally, he had a few stories regarding the phase of kingdom work called stewardship. One I thought was priceless. It went something like this:

A congregation was planning to build a new church. They needed $10,000 more to start with the first phase.

A parishioner decided to contribute the ten thousand, but he told the pastor that he did not want anyone to know that he was making that contribution.

The next Sunday, the pastor announced that they finally had enough to start building. He said also that the man who made the $10,000 contribution needed to get started wanted to remain anonymous.

At that moment, the man who made the contribution stood up and said, "I thought it would be better that way."

Manny had a story for any subject and all occasions, and he always made sure that the story taught a lesson.

I'm sure that everyone who attended that Fourth of July church picnic at Trinity Church in 1943 remembers well how a beautiful day turned to tragedy in a moment! Certainly, no one in our family could forget it because the tragedy hit so close to home, causing such serious injury to our brother.

Although dear brother Manny was injured so badly that day in 1943 and had problems the rest of his life because of it, with God's help, he kept his life going in a positive way and served the Lord to the best of his ability.

CHAPTER TWENTY-SIX

OUR FATHER, THE *SEHLSORGER*
(Carer Of Souls)

In the chapter about how I started to *prepare for the ministry* when I was a young boy, I say that a man told me, when I was about nine, that if I would become half of the *Sehlsorger* (carer for souls) that my father was, I'd be a good pastor when I would grow up.

I felt proud of my father when I heard that. (Though I was so young, I had told the man that I hoped I'd be a pastor someday.) I truly felt that my father was very much *a man of God.* In fact, as I have said, when as a child, I saw him in a worship service chanting the benediction in German with his hands "over the congregation," I felt that he could have parted the Red Sea like Moses did with the Lord working through him.

I knew Dad was not perfect; he always said "*we* sinners," not just "*you*" when speaking from the pulpit. However, I was sure that he was especially chosen by God to be His servant.

He may not have been the greatest pulpit orator, but he preached the Word—the Law and Gospel—very well, and he practiced what he preached to the best of his ability.

He was certainly a Bible scholar. In fact, it almost seemed that he had the Bible memorized. He even knew the Old Testament about as well as we kids knew the words to "Jesus loves me." Also, he knew how to apply the scriptures in various circumstances of life.

His forte, though, was his being a *people person*. He would be the first to tell you that he was just an *undershepherd helping the Good Shepherd*, but I know that he was a *good* undershepherd, if that's what he was, especially in his relationship with people.

He could talk to anyone, anywhere, and he related well to his parishioners. He truly *rejoiced with them when they rejoiced* and *wept with them when they wept*, though he did not always *display* a great deal of emotion in difficult situations.

For example, at the saddest of funerals, I never saw him shed tears. Nor did he get choked up at a baptism, confirmation, wedding, or ordination, *even when it involved one of his own children*. It was always obvious how he felt, however.

When he was asked in an interview, at about age seventy, how he wanted to be remembered, he said he'd like to be remembered simply as a carer of souls (*Sehlsorger*, in German). That, I do believe he was—very much a carer of souls. Our father showed that so many times in so many ways.

I think of one day, in particular. It was the day a one-room school was totally destroyed by a tornado with a young teacher and about a dozen children in it. It happened in April of 1942. I'll never forget the day, nor the things said in praise of our father regarding that day.

I was in the eighth grade. Marty, Manny, Danny, and I were in school at Odessa. It was a terribly stormy day. From the Odessa school, which was on a hill, some of us students watched a number of tails form in the threatening, low-hanging clouds off in the distance. We were sure that tornadoes were forming in those clouds, and we were fearful that one might come our way and hit our school or the town of Odessa.

That didn't happen, but one of those terribly violent, powerful *whirlwinds in the sky* did hit a small school near the state line between Minnesota and South Dakota, about ten miles southeast of Ortonville, seven or eight miles west of Odessa.

The teacher in that school, Edna May, was one of Dad's parishioners from Odessa. She was only twenty-two at the time, the youngest daughter of Paul Mays, who were also members of Trinity in Odessa. The May family farm was a few miles north of Odessa.

In addition to the young teacher being a member of a church Dad served, one of the pupils, Dorothy Laskowsky, was from one of the families in the church Dad served in Yellow Bank.

I've never been close to a tornado, but I have several times seen the aftermath of those terribly destructive storms. The storm that hit that little school that day was a very bad one.

It so thoroughly destroyed the school that there was hardly a piece of the building left intact—only the concrete foundation. Two children were killed, and a number of the others were seriously injured, including the young teacher.

I interviewed Edna May in Bellingham, where she lived in her later years, several years before she went to be with the Lord. She shared with me many things that she remembered from that day.

It is not my intention to tell you all what Edna told me, except to say that she was very thankful to the Lord for my father's ministering to her and others that day. She told me that Dad was very much the compassionate pastor in that circumstance, ministering like *an angel of mercy* to members of his fold and to others—some of them people he had never met.

Edna said it was as though Dad was sent by the Lord Himself to take the injured and the traumatized by the hand and to pray with them and assure them that the Lord was with them. She said that our father's presence there, so soon after the tragedy occurred, was as though it was a part of the whole experience.

The ministering to the Laskowsky family, too, was greatly appreciated, and it was far from a simple matter. Not only was ten-year-old Dorothy Laskowsky, one of the injured pupils who was found some distance from the school, but also *Dorothy's father had the horrible experience of seeing it all happen!*

The terrible storm hit the school *just twenty minutes before it would have been time for the afternoon dismissal. Ervin Laskowsky, who was on his way to the school to take his daughter home, saw the tornado hit the school!*

He saw the tornado take the mud and water from a pond in a nearby barnyard and slam it onto the school as it twisted everything to bits. Most of the children and the teacher had stayed seated or had lain flat on the floor. Two of the pupils, however, had gotten up to close the door and a window. Those two were killed.

Mr. Laskowsky, Dorothy's father, was tremendously traumatized by the experience. It was extremely difficult for him to have watched it happen. I was told by the teacher, Edna May, that our father was like a messenger from God to give Ervin Laskowsky strength and assure him of the Lord's presence.

One of the reasons why I cite this example of Dad's being a special carer for souls that day is that, in fact, he was in no physical condition to be there.

Earlier that afternoon, Dad had most of his teeth pulled by an oral surgeon in Ortonville. When he came home from the dentist, we had just gotten home from school. We told him what had happened at that state-line school. I remember well how Dad was getting out of the car in the parsonage driveway, holding a cloth to his aching jaw. He was obviously in terrible pain.

I'll never forget how he looked. He was still bleeding from the oral surgery and in pain. Though in misery, he said, when he heard what happened to that little school and the people in it, "I'd better get out there as soon as I can."

Mother pleaded with him to call a pastor in Ortonville to see if he would go out there in his place. However, though he was in pain and his jaw was swollen, he went in the house to wash up to go.

Although he was going against our mother's better judgment, she insisted on going with him. She did, but she did not drive, so he had to do that too. Marcia also went along, but she wasn't old enough to drive.

I didn't accompany them because the *Star-Journal* papers had just arrived and had to be delivered. Of course, being two years younger than Marty, I wasn't old enough to drive either.

Marcia and mother said that it was as though Dad totally forgot about his own physical discomfort as he ministered to the people at the scene of the tragedy and later at the hospital in Ortonville. Marty said, though, that Dad did have trouble speaking at times because of his missing teeth.

Later that evening, after Dad was home again, he was in such misery that Mom wanted him to be taken to the hospital himself.

Dad rejected the idea, however, because he did not want anyone to know about the personal problem he had while he was ministering to the victims of the tornado.

Dad, it seems to me, showed that day as he always did in his ministry what a true *Sehlsorger* (carer of souls) he was!

I think of one more example of the many times and many ways Dad's showed special compassion in his ministry. No, this didn't involve his ministering to people in a crisis, like the tornado. What I'm thinking of, rather, had to do with his relationship with young people. Although it was not a tragedy, it was a crisis to the young people involved.

In 1943, the Odessa High School basketball team was scheduled to play in a district tournament on Ash Wednesday. Little Odessa was not always invited to play in the district tournament. That year was special because the team had done well. The team was honored, and the whole high school was excited about it.

The problem was that most of the team members, several of the cheerleaders, and many of the students who wanted to go to the game were members of Trinity Luthcran Church. Why would this be a problem? Because a special service with Holy Communion was always conducted on that evening—Ash Wednesday.

Some of the older members of the church could not imagine how *good Christian people* could miss an Ash Wednesday communion service for a basketball game, no matter who was playing!

Dad, of course, found out what the fuss was all about, so he decided to give an alternative choice to all those who were on the team and others who wanted to attend the tournament Ash Wednesday evening in Granite Falls. Dad arranged to have a devotion—with communion—at the time of the dismissal from school that day, about 2:00 PM.

The devotion at the church was well attended, and everyone seemed pleased with the way things turned out. Most of the people gave Dad credit for the way he handled the matter.

The team lost the game that evening in the final seconds, but at least they couldn't imagine that the Lord was against them. After all, *they had not missed the Ash Wednesday communion service!*

When I was a college teacher, I had a card that said, "Students don't care how much you know until they know how much you care." I put it over my desk as a reminder because I think it is so true. I know that is so true of a pastor's relationship with his people too. *The parishioners don't care how much their pastor knows until they know how much he cares.*

Our father's caring relationship with young people was also shown in his sense of humor. As serious as he was about his ministry, especially when Dad was around youth, there was always good-natured laughter. He kidded with them, and of course, the kidding went the other way too.

For example, one spring Sunday afternoon when I was with him as he was driving toward the rural church he served, he stopped near a bridge over the Minnesota River where the water was running over the road. Nearby were several boys from the Odessa congregation spearing carp near the bridge.

After Dad joked with the boys, whom he knew well, about their fishing skills, he asked one of them if it was safe to drive through the water that was running over the road. One of them said, "You can drive through there, Reverend, as long as you don't disturb the fish."

Dad laughed, and we drove through the flooded area and on toward Yellow Bank. When we arrived at the Yellow Bank church, one of the men approached our car and said, "Well, Pastor, I see you drove through the river on your way out here."

Dad responded with a smile, "It wasn't that bad. We drove through the water running over the road without a problem. It wasn't that deep."

"Is that right?" the man asked. "What is this here?" There, wedged between the front bumper and the grill of our '36 Chevy, was a large fish. Obviously, the boys who were spearing carp in the Minnesota River put it there as a joke.

During the war, there was evidence too of Dad's relationship with young people. Soldiers, of which there were many during World War II, always stopped to visit Dad when they were home on furlough.

Dad enjoyed those visits and always loved to hear them talk of their experiences and offered them encouragement. Any number of the servicemen also wrote to Dad from various parts of the world, and he always answered every letter—in his beautiful longhand.

Dad may not have been a tremendous scholar the way it is viewed by the learned of the secular world, but that didn't matter to most people who knew him, especially his parishioners.

To those who called him pastor, I think it was true *that they didn't care about how much he knew, as long as they knew how much he cared.* He did care; that I know. If he was anything, he was a *Sehlsorger* (carer of souls).

CHAPTER TWENTY-SEVEN

COTTON BLOSSOM SINGERS AT TRINITY CHURCH

In winter of 1936, our pastor father received a letter from a school called Piney Woods in Mississippi. The letter, from one of the school administrators, explained that the finest singing group from their school called the "Cotton Blossom Singers" was going to be on tour in the Midwest that summer.

Then there was a request for the group to present *an evening of Christian songs* at our church. There was no mention of the singers being Negro, but a photo included with the letter showed that all members of the group were black.

They said the group had their own transportation and a bus house to live in. The means of transportation and "house" they lived in was on the picture of the group.

Dad talked it over with the elders of our church. The men thought it sounded like an interesting evening to have for the church, so they wrote their affirmative answer.

The group, a quartette and their manager, arrived in early summer of 1937. Shortly after the men arrived, they showed us their bus house, which was obviously homemade and not very big. (A photo taken in our yard of their bus is included in the picture section of this book.) When my father and mother saw the cramped quarters in the bus house, they invited the men to stay with us in our house.

In the summer of 1937, we in our family were all at home, but at our house, it seemed our parents always thought there was room for a few more. Our folks gave the singers our beds, and several of us boys slept on the floor.

The evening of song was well attended; all the people enjoyed the concert and were enthusiastic about the singers. Until then, everything seemed to be all right.

However, when people in the town and in the congregation found out that members of our family had given black people our beds, there was some adverse criticism. Some of the things said weren't very nice at all, especially what some said about us and our attitude toward those people.

To my parents *these men were guests,* and guests were usually given beds, and members of the family would sleep on the floor.

We boys certainly didn't mind. That's the way it was when we had guests in the house, no matter who they were—relatives, friends, or anyone invited to stay with us.

When our parents, in fact, found out that the Cotton Blossom Singers had other places in our area to sing, they invited the men to make our place their home base. So the members of the quartette stayed with us for more than a week.

Ihno even drove them to several of the places they sang, even as far away as Hastings, Minnesota, south of St. Paul.

Some of the criticism became a little sharp after that. It was hard for us to imagine why. The men were *our guests*. Why should anyone question who we invited to stay with us, or with whom Ihno would travel?

One afternoon, several of the members of the Cotton Blossom Singers played softball with us and a number of the kids in the town. They were good players—really good ballplayers, and they were fun to have playing with us.

The next day we also asked them to play basketball with us on our backyard "court." Our basket and backboard weren't the greatest; they were on the side of our barn. Those men were excellent basketball players too. In fact, they could clown around with the basketball and pass to each other in really fun ways.

What was interesting was that the boys from the town who played with us were very much impressed by the singers' ability, their friendliness, and their sportsmanship.

Several of the boys from town remarked about how much fun they had and what great guys these men were. I never heard any of those boys refer to them in any other way than *men, singers, or good ballplayers*.

Not one of the boys referred to the quartette members by their color or race. In fact, there was not a negative thing said by any of the boys in any way. It seems that they all came to think of them as other human beings and friends. All the boys liked them.

The boys also called the members of the singing group by their names. One of them, I remember, was named Bostic, and one was called "Stringbean" by his fellow singers. He was tall and lean, so it seemed like a fitting name for him.

The boys in our town enjoyed calling him "Stringbean." They thought that was kind of funny, and they got to like the man very much. He was the most comical of all them, and he was really a fancy ball handler, especially with the basketball.

Word got around, I guess, that the boys from town enjoyed being with the singers, and it seemed to change the attitude of some of the townspeople about the men.

In fact, another day, when the boys and the singers played basketball, some of the men from the town came to watch, and they talked with the singers afterward. Then, it seemed, the men from Mississippi were just visitors in the town; it wasn't like they were *people from outer space or anything like that.*

Our dad commented at dinner in our house one evening that it was interesting how people's attitude had changed. "At first," Dad said to the singers, "it was like you were strangers, different from the people here in the town. It's interesting now that they regard you as friends."

One of the men commented on how they liked being treated like *God's children* rather than as people who were different.

It was indeed interesting to see how the attitude of the people changed after they got to know them a little bit. Of course, there were a few people who didn't change their attitude. Dad said you can't change some people who are so set in their ways, like some old Germans who think their blood is a different color.

Manny and I were pretty young at that time; in the summer of 1937, I was eight, and Manny was six. I was told, though I do not remember this: Both Manny and I *prayed* after the men left that God would make us black because *we thought that would make us better basketball players*. Also, we thought if God would answer our prayers, *we would be able to sing like they did*.

CHAPTER TWENTY-EIGHT

MY SPECIAL FOURTH OF JULY

The "bombs burst in air . . ."—at the wrong time.

When I was a child, in the 1930s and early '40s, it seemed that the summers revolved around the Fourth of July. The day was special because it was *Independence Day*, our special national day! Everyone knew that—every man, woman and child!

It was never "observed" on any other day. *The fourth was the fourth*, no matter what day of the week it was. Businesses were closed, and people took the day off from work and had picnics and social gatherings.

In the village of Odessa, it was no different; the Fourth of July was the fourth. And even though our little village was a long way from where the War for Independence was fought in the eighteenth century, our independence was associated with fireworks. In Odessa, of course, there was no fireworks display, like there was in large cities, but we kids bought firecrackers to have our own fun.

Unfortunately, there was always danger connected with that fun. One time, in 1940, I think it was, we bought some good-sized *bangers* from Kollitz's store for half price on the morning of the fourth (end-of-the-season sale, I guess). In midmorning, Manny and I went over to Gimmestads, near downtown. There, Corky and George Gimmestad joined us in using what we had just purchased.

We lit some of the big firecrackers under empty cans for a while. Then we got brave and started to light the firecrackers in our hands and threw them into a big mud puddle in their barnyard. What fun!

Yes, it was fun, seeing the muddy water fly into the air as each firecracker exploded on its surface—until something disastrous happened.

Usually, as the wick on a firecracker was lit, we had about a second till the device would explode. That gave us enough time to throw it into the puddle. We were good at it—fast is the word! Nothing would happen to us; *we were fast!*

Even when the wicks were not twisted as tight as they should have been, as long as we had a split second between lighting the wick and throwing it, nothing would happen. We were quick! When the time for the wick to burn was reduced to almost no time at all, we'd still make it! So we thought.

All of a sudden, I lit the wick of a big one! "*Pssstt! BANG!*" It exploded in my hand, right next to my right shoulder, before I had time to get rid of it! The boys looked aghast! There I was, looking at my hand, badly burned and bloody! How could this happen? We were fast! But it did happen!

There was blood all over me—my head, my hair, and my shirt, my overalls, even on my face!

My first instinct was to run home. I took off running as fast as I could, and Manny followed! I knew what Dad and Mom would say, but I was hurt—badly hurt! What they would say didn't seem to matter at the moment! I needed help! It felt like my hand was coming off! It was so painful!

The five minutes it usually took to run that far was cut in half, I'm sure! When I got near our house, I saw Uncle Ted Thormahlen's car and remembered that he was there! That made matters worse! What Dad would say would be bad enough! But having Uncle Ted Thormahlen there multiplied the problem! He knew everything—at least he thought he did! And Uncle Ted knew what a perfect parent should be because he was one; at least *he* thought so!

There wasn't time for a confession! I showed Dad my hand! What Dad said to me when he saw it almost hurt more than the terrible wound, but he called Mother and they tried to figure out what to do!

What Uncle Ted said, however, multiplied the pain by a thousand! Uncle Ted, *"the know it all"* lit into me like he was the Lord of all! He even blamed Dad for allowing me to have firecrackers! My hand didn't seem to bother him! *His opinion* was what counted!

Dad had not *allowed us* to have firecrackers; Manny and I had taken matters into our own hands (no pun intended). It wasn't Dad's fault at all, but Uncle Ted always had to put Dad down in one way or another.

Had Uncle Ted had his family with him, I'm sure that cousin David would have been with us. I wonder what Uncle would have said had it been cousin David who'd had his hand blown apart!

Anyway, Dad got the car out and took me to the doctor in Ortonville. Uncle Ted came along! I was wishing he'd have stayed at our house. He could have tried to calm down Mom, his older sister! She was almost hysterical! But then, maybe it was better that he went with us. Mom would have wanted to shoot her dear critical brother, if he'd have gotten after her like he did Dad!

On the way to Ortonville, Dad, who was not the world's best driver, was all over the road while Uncle Ted went on haranguing at him. Actually, I think I felt the pain less while feeling sorry for Dad to have to take all that from Uncle Ted.

When we got to the Ortonville hospital, Dr. Bolsta had to take some of Uncle Ted's guff too! Dear old Dr. Bolsta! I think he wanted to stick a needle in Uncle Ted to knock him out or at least sew up his mouth! Instead, he made Uncle Ted wait in the waiting room. That temporarily helped the doctor as well as Dad and me.

After the doctor fixed me up the best he could and gave Dad instructions how to care for the wound in the next days, we headed back to Odessa. As you might know, Uncle Ted continued the barrage of negativism toward Dad and me all the way back to Odessa. By the time we arrived at home, I began to wonder whether my name was really *Dumme Esel (dumb donkey)*.

The next morning, the pain in my hand had somewhat subsided; Uncle Ted left. Dad, I'm sure, was as relieved as I was. Even our mother, although she loved her brother, was not too sorry to see him get on his way.

The Apostle Paul said, "All things work together for good to those who love God." There certainly were some salutary effects of this stupid mistake of mine with the big firecracker that day.

For one thing, I learned to appreciate Dad more and thanked God sincerely that *he* was my father and not Theodore Thormahlen!

Also, I became determined that day that I would never try to *know everything*—for sure, not more than a pastor in Odessa, or a doctor in Ortonville!

Another bit of good that came of this stupid mistake of mine was that I learned a little more German that day because almost everything said by Dad and Uncle Ted was *auf Deutsch*.

One more thing was that I learned to be more *ambidextrous* because my right hand was bandaged most of the rest of the summer. I even tried writing with my left hand in the remainder of the summer school confirmation classes.

I really learned how to use my left hand for painting. (A part of my *"sentence"* was to paint the back porch and a few other things.) I also learned how to play ball fairly well with one hand—my left. I even used the bat with just my left hand and got a few hits, believe it or not.

I'm very thankful to this day that my right hand healed so well. The palm of my hand and my split and burned fingers peeled and peeled in the healing process until after school started in the fall. I carry almost no scars on my hand; it healed so well, thank God! To be sure, *I learned to let the professionals make us recall "the bombs bursting in air" to appreciate our country's independence.* I vowed that day never to light another firecracker!

I had no permanent damage, however, from my Fourth of July stupidity that day. Maybe the Lord thought I endured enough that day listening to Uncle Ted; I didn't need anything more to realize that. *Dumme Esel* that I might have been that day, I was sure that it wasn't a permanent condition.

CHAPTER TWENTY-NINE

SUMMER BIBLE SCHOOL IN ODESSA AND YELLOW BANK

When I was a child, our pastor father taught summer school classes in both Odessa and Yellow Bank for six weeks during June and July. The classes, primarily for the confirmands, were held at Trinity in Odessa from nine to twelve on weekdays.

When there were confirmands in Yellow Bank, their classes were held in the afternoons Monday through Friday. The classes in Odessa were held in the little schoolhouse on the church property. In Yellow Bank, the classes met in the schoolroom in the old parsonage.

Most of the children in Odessa rode their bicycles to these classes, some as far as seven or eight miles. I remember seeing a picture of about fifteen kids on bikes on the school grounds. Our brother Danny is in front of them on a tricycle. It looks like Danny was probably five years old, which would mean that the picture was taken about 1939.

Our sister Ruth is on the photo. During the school year, at that time, she taught at a Lutheran school in the Montevideo area. In the summer, she was very likely helping Dad teach those of us who were younger while he taught the confirmands.

I was one of the younger ones at that time. It was fun to have Ruth teach us; she was a very creative teacher. Dad was a good teacher too, but he was kind of *old school* in his methods.

There was a lot of memorization in the teaching of both the confirmands and the younger children. All of us learned to *rattle off* passages of Scripture as fast as anyone could listen to them. It was good also to know not only *what* we believed but where it was from in the Bible. We were proud to show that all teaching of the Lutheran Church was based *on God's Word in the Bible.*

In the Odessa summer sessions, Dad always gave the children a half-hour recess in the middle of the morning. We usually played a short game of kitten ball (softball) "work up" during that time. While we played, Dad usually went to the parsonage to have a cup of coffee.

When Dad came out to call us back into the school, the boys would tell Dad that it was *his turn to bat*. Dad wasn't much of an *athlete*, but he was a good *sport*. He'd take "his turn to bat," like the boys wanted him to. He knew very well that what the boys really wanted was *a little longer recess*, but he went along with it.

When Dad had classes to teach in the afternoon at Yellow Bank, we younger kids in the family would often go with him, especially if he would offer to take us for a swim in the Yellow Bank River after the classes.

The Yellow Bank River wasn't a great place to swim, but we went to a special place on a bend of the river near the mission festival grounds where it was a little deeper. Good place or not, it was enjoyable to be with Dad. He was a lot of fun at these times, and he was very gentle with us.

Also, he had an unusual way to swim, which he had learned growing up in Germany. He could even swim with one of the smaller of us kids on his back. That was usually little Danny, the youngest in our family, who was probably no more than five at the time.

In addition to these classes in the summer, Dad taught the confirmands also on Tuesdays and Thursday afternoons from two thirty to four o'clock. This was release time from public school. Confirmands who didn't attend public school in Odessa were brought into town by their parents at that time from the country schools.

Most of the students were pretty faithful in attending these classes, and they usually did the assignments Dad gave them. The Bible and Luther's Small Catechism were the textbooks for all these classes along with the additional notes Dad prepared and dictated to us.

Confirmation day was usually *Palm Sunday* (the Sunday before Easter) each year, unless Easter was very early. That was a special day for the entire congregation, but it was a *very special* day for the confirmands and their families.

In the worship service on confirmation day, those to be confirmed were questioned by Dad in front of the congregation for about forty-five minutes.

The class was seated in front of the church sanctuary, facing the altar. Our father paced slowly in front of the students while he did the questioning. The classes were usually from eight or nine to fifteen in number. Following confirmation was first communion.

The reason the confirmands were examined was to show the congregation that they knew the basis of Christian doctrine from the Bible. The most important was the Law and the Gospel. It was emphasized that a person who is a Christian must *understand well and believe* firmly that *the Law shows our sin and the Gospel shows our salvation.*

It was also very important to understand and firmly believe what the Scripture says of the Sacraments—Baptism and The Lord's Supper.

Confirmation was in fact the *confirming of the baptismal vow.* The young people, usually about fourteen years old (ordinarily in the eighth grade) were announcing publicly that they believed that the Triune God—the Father, Son, and Holy Spirit—was the God of the universe, that the Bible was His Word for the world, and that Jesus was the Messiah, prophesied of old, to come to the world.

It was very important that the confirmands confess that *Jesus Christ was their Savior* and vow to remain faithful to Him until death.

If you ask Lutherans who were questioned in front of the congregation on Confirmation Day if it was difficult, they will tell you in no uncertain terms that it indeed was!

They will, however, also tell you that it was a good experience, one they will not forget. It's interesting, also, how most of those who were confirmed usually remember what they were taught for the rest of their life.

I like to tell people that there is one thing more difficult than being questioned for confirmation in front of the congregation, and that is to be *questioned by your father* in front of the congregation on confirmation day!

I saw it when my older brothers and sisters were confirmed, and I experienced it myself: when others in the class faltered in answering, Dad would call on his son or daughter in the class.

I know, because I was called on a number of times, when my classmates faltered the day we were confirmed. Dad was always very understanding toward those who had trouble at times in answering. He knew it was most often because they were nervous being in front of the congregation.

I'll never forget my confirmation day. It was Palm Sunday of 1942, which that year was March 29. I recall very well how I vowed to remain faithful to the Lord all my life.

I think we were all determined to do just that: remain faithful to the Lord!

Lutherans are not taught that only Lutherans are God's people. They are taught, rather, that *faith in the*

Lord Jesus Christ is what makes a person a Christian, and they are taught that they should be loyal to Him for their salvation.

I suppose that most Lutherans stay faithful to the Lord because of the solid Bible teaching they have received, especially if they were taught as children. It is also very important that they are taught to strive to live according to the commandments, in appreciation to the Lord for His love and grace.

I know it was not easy for Dad to teach the summer school classes for six weeks, both in Odessa and in Yellow Bank. It was, however, very worthwhile for the children who were taught. For that matter, I don't recall that people complained about attending the classes.

When my father meets in heaven, those he taught in the many confirmation classes over the years, there surely is rejoicing among the angels that they remained faithful to the Lord through their lifetime.

CHAPTER THIRTY

HOW WELL I REMEMBER DECEMBER 7, 1941!

December 7, 1941, began like any other Sunday for us in the village of Odessa, Minnesota. Little did we know when we were in church and Sunday School that **all hell was about to break loose**—not just *for us*, but for the entire world.

I was thirteen; sister Marcia was two years older, my brother Manny two years younger. What a day that turned out to be! However, we knew nothing of what was happening in the Pacific until we came home from skating on the Minnesota River late in the afternoon.

Where we lived, in Western Minnesota, it was cold that December day—probably no more fifteen degrees above zero at noon. It was a bright sunny day; however, a good day to go skating, we thought.

After Dad and Mom left for the afternoon worship service in Yellow Bank, taking seven-year-old Danny with them, Marty, Manny, and I set out with a few friends for the Minnesota River.

The place on the river where we usually skated was about a mile from the village, about a half-hour walk over the school hill.

The ice was almost perfect; the river had evidently frozen over with no snow falling on the water as it froze. A little snow had fallen Saturday night, making the whole scene almost a *winter wonderland.* There wasn't enough snow on the ice, though, to bother our skating.

Some of the boys built a warming fire, but as active as we were, it wasn't really necessary. Also, we were all accustomed to the conditions and were very well dressed for the cold. In fact, we sometimes joked about being *Minnesota Eskimos.*

We had a great afternoon, racing, playing tag, forming chains of skaters for playing "crack the whip," and trying some figure skating "competition." Some of us even skated all the way over to the Cold Spring granite quarry, about a mile down the river.

On our way to the quarry, we passed by the bend in the river where we often went fishing for bullheads in the summer. Manny wondered whether there were any of those obstinate thorny headed fish under the ice that afternoon, glad that we were skating rather than trying to *"hook them into coming home with us for dinner."*

About four o'clock, the shadows were getting longer as the sun was going down. The smallest stones on the riverbank cast shadows, and the rabbits we saw cast shadows several feet long.

We joked and laughed as we changed from skates to boots to start home, and we were a happy-go-lucky group of kids all the way back to the village.

We parted from the others at the bottom of the school hill and headed for the parsonage where we lived. Though we were a bit tired and hungry as we arrived, we still had happy faces.

As we opened the back door of our house, however, our looks changed; Dad's face told us something was wrong.

He related immediately what had happened at Pearl Harbor in Hawaii just hours earlier. We asked him what this meant for our country. As he told us, we cried and hugged him and our mother, wondering what was happening in the world. We knew there was war in Europe, but we had hoped and prayed that it would end before our country would be involved.

After we got our jackets and boots off, Dad explained more of what happened; then we all sat close to the radio. After supper, Dad led us in a devotion and prayer. How he pleaded with God for peace and for guidance for our country's leaders!

While we were still at the table, our father stated that this surely would mean that the United States would be brought into the war, which, he said, would probably become another *world* war.

Dad was from Germany, but he had said for some time, that it was his opinion that, if the United States did not join Great Britain and the Allied Forces, the Germans, under the Hitler, may defeat them. Dad did not want to see that happen; he said that German domination of Europe would be an utter disaster.

Although his parents and all his relatives were still in Germany, Dad didn't like what was happening with the Nazis at the helm.

He had come to America before the last world war because he did not like the political situation at that time under the Kaiser.

He had an even *more* fearful distrust of *Hitler*. He had read *Mein Kampf* and others of Hitler's writings (in German) and listened to the Nazis' speeches on shortwave radio. He knew they wanted to rule the world and *would do just that* if given a chance. He shook his head in disgust each time he thought about that.

I was in eighth grade in December of 1941; Marty was in tenth. The day after the attack on Pearl Harbor, Monday, December 8, we did little more in school than read the morning papers, look at maps, listen to the radio, and discuss with our teachers what was happening. We also heard President Roosevelt's speech to the U.S. joint session of Congress on radio that morning, in which he said that December 7, 1941, would *"live in infamy."*

There was nothing but news of the war on the radio, and we listened through most of the school day. The Odessa school superintendent, Mr. Pagel, who was very much *up on world affairs*, led some of the discussions.

Mr. Pagel and our father were good friends and frequently discussed what was going on in the world. Mr.

Pagel was of German descent and in fact, taught a German class at Odessa High School. He was born in the United States, but he, like our dad, had relatives in Germany. Mr. Pagel and our father sometimes sat for hours in Dad's study discussing world affairs.

Interestingly, our father had said to some of his friends *the week before December 7* that it was his opinion that if the United States didn't get into the war *over the Atlantic*, the nation may become involved in the war *over the Pacific*.

Our father was of the opinion that the United States should join the Allied Forces to keep the Nazis from defeating them. Also, Dad was well aware of *the alliances Hitler had made with the Japanese* who were trying to dominate Asia.

Because he had said that, about the possibility of our getting involved *over the Pacific,* he was severely criticized by some people for *knowing more than he should*. Dad didn't *know* what was going to happen; he was just extremely perceptive.

In the weeks after the United States declared war on Germany, our father was suspected by some *superpatriots* of being a traitor. They accused him because of his German heritage and because he was quite outspoken about world affairs. Also, Dad was critical of President Roosevelt's domestic as well as foreign policies.

Also, of course, some of the worship services in the churches Dad served were conducted in German. Many of the people in that part of Minnesota and eastern

South Dakota were of German descent and still used that language, especially in their homes and in their spiritual life.

Someone, who I guess thought that all people who spoke German were suddenly enemies of the United States, painted a crude *swastika* on the church door next to the parsonage where we lived.

At that time too, Dad started to receive strange, *anonymous* letters, accusing him of disloyalty. There were also suspicious visitors at our house at times who spoke German and acted like they were trying to trap Dad somehow. Fortunately, Dad could speak enough Norwegian and Danish to fake it with *those nuts*. Finally, they left him alone.

Well, I didn't mean for this chapter to get into the months that followed the attack on Pearl Harbor. I just meant to recall that fateful December Sunday in 1941 and the days that followed.

Getting involved in the war changed everyone's life in one way or another. Also, a lot of young men, including our brother Vernon; our uncle, Walter Thormaehlen; and cousins Lothar and Willard Mueller, were soon serving our nation in various parts of the world. In fact, not long after December of 1941, almost every young man, except some farm boys, was serving in the military forces.

Our sister Anita married a man who was born and partly brought up in Germany. He too had some accusations of disloyalty just because of his heritage, but he joined the U.S. army and served almost all during the war.

December 7, 1941, turned the whole world upside down and changed the life of all of us. How quickly even children can go from carefree skating on a peaceful river in Western Minnesota to being affected by chaotic international affairs!

CHAPTER THIRTY-ONE

FARM WORK IS BEST DONE BY FARMERS

Starting when we were about eight and ten years old, Manny and I did a lot of yard work in the summers. We especially mowed lawns and worked in people's gardens. The lawn mowing was always done by a push reel-type mower; that's all we had. Sometimes we both had to push together, and at times, we'd put a rope on the front so one of us could pull while the other pushed.

Most of the time we got from twenty-five to thirty-five cents (together) for a lawn that took us a couple of hours. We always hoped that the lady of the house would do the paying, rather than the man, because we usually got a little more from the woman. The lady of the house sometimes even gave us milk and cookies in the middle of the morning or afternoon.

When we got a little older, though, farm work was the only other thing available to us as a summer job around Odessa. We were too young and didn't weigh enough to work at a granite quarry or with a section crew on the railroad. I worked on a number of farms, starting when I was about twelve years old.

Farm work never fascinated me, though it was a way to earn something. I always thought the only ones who could really *like* to do farm work would be the farmers themselves and their families. They had a personal interest in the crops and the animals. We made the best of it, though, and the farm families were always good to us.

The first farm job I had for pay was in 1941 when I was going on thirteen. I drove tractor for haying and threshing. The days were pretty long and the pay was only a dollar a day and room and board. I didn't mind it so much, though, because I rather enjoyed driving a tractor. A tractor didn't go as fast as I would have liked it to, but it was at least *going, and I was doing the driving!*

Also, the room at the farmhouse was all right, and the meals were very good. Those farmer families really knew how to eat! Besides preparing a good breakfast, dinner, and supper, the women even came out to the fields with a morning lunch about 9:30 AM and an afternoon lunch about 4:00 PM.

I caused a little excitement one day, though, when I tipped over with a narrow front-wheel John Deere tractor. I was driving on the crest of a hill on Highway 12, north of Odessa, when I saw cars coming *sixty miles per hour* from both directions.

From the crest of the hill, I could see both of them, but it seemed like they probably didn't see each other. I figured that they could hit head-on if I didn't get out of the way. Just as I headed for the ditch, the cars met and passed, probably without seeing me or the John Deere I was on.

The ditch I headed into was a little deep. As the tractor hit the bottom, with those narrow front wheels, it rolled over. Fortunately, I jumped clear as the tractor was tipping, and I was able to get the engine turned off before a fire could start from the leaking gas.

The tractor wasn't damaged at all, and the farmer was pleased that I wasn't hurt either. In fact, when I explained what happened, I even got a little praise for my getting out of the way of the cars.

There had been several accidents that summer in Western Minnesota caused by cars turning out for slow-moving farm machinery on the highway. In fact, there was one very bad accident earlier that summer on Highway 75 just a mile out of Odessa. Two cars hit head-on as one of them was trying to miss a farm machine coming out of driveway of a farm. I think about ten people were killed in that tragedy.

One interesting thing about the Norwegian farmer, whose John Deere I rolled over, was how he'd say in the morning, after breakfast, with his heavy Norwegian accent and singsong lilt, "*Ya, darn it, then, let's get something done.*"

Then, after a few hours of work, about eleven thirty, he'd say, "*Well, darn it, then, let's go listen to 'Ma Perkins.'*" That was a half-hour, *soap-opera*-type radio program that he and his wife listened to on a battery-powered radio. (They didn't have electricity.)

The next summer, I worked for another farmer, riding and operating the binder for cutting the grain and tying it into bundles. The pay for that was two dollars a day. Then later, when I helped shock the grain bundles for that farmer, I earned forty cents an hour. I thought I was doing pretty well. And of course, on top of that, I got room and board.

The next summer I worked pitching bundles for threshing. Before the summer was over, the pay had gone up to a dollar an hour due to the shortage of farm workers during World War II. That was pretty good pay for farm work. At least, I thought so.

There were a number of migrant workers on the threshing crew that summer. I didn't mind working with them, but I got a lot of razzing from them because they knew that I attended a ministerial prep school in St. Paul.

I got a special amount of ribbing one day when I fell off the perch seat into a load of flax, causing a runaway with a team of horses. (The story of the runaway horses is told in another chapter of this book.)

The evening after that happened, I heard some interesting stories about what some of the men said they had experienced with runaway horses. I listened, but I wondered how much of what they were telling was true.

Work and life went on after that. I made enough that summer, at a dollar an hour, to pay my board and room at prep school for both the fall and spring semesters—$250! It was nice during that school year to have my room and board paid. That way, when I earned a little doing yard work and housework at homes near the prep school, I was actually able to keep the money; I didn't have to use it to pay for my schooling.

When I had to work off my room and board at the school, I worked in the school kitchen, or in the maintenance department for about thirty cents an hour. And I never even received the pay; it was just applied to my room and board.

For several months one year, I washed dishes for ten cents a meal. That wasn't much, but when I washed dishes, I got to eat with the kitchen employees, which was nice; they always had a little more to eat.

Part of the last summer, I did farm work in the Odessa area; we had working with us a few rather *rough and tumble farmhands* from Texas. They liked to taunt me at times because I was a student. They frequently made me the butt of jokes during the day, calling me *college boy egghead* or "*wannabe professor.*"

However, after work in the evening, or on rainy mornings when it was too wet to thresh grain, a couple of those guys who were more or less functionally illiterate asked me to write letters for them.

They especially liked it when I helped them write to their girlfriends with poetic thoughts, like, "*The stars I see as I lie here tonight make me think of your beautiful eyes,*" or, "*the sweet smell in the breeze this morning reminds me of the fragrance in your silky hair,*" and things like that. I had fun writing flowery stuff for them, and they loved it.

After I helped them write to their parents and girlfriends a few times, I got a little less static from them during the day. Some of them even asked me serious questions after that, especially if one of them was with me alone, apart from the other guys.

Those men really didn't know much of what was happening in the world, or even in the United States. I made sure, though, that I didn't show off with knowledge or make fun of them. I think some of the men who said they were from Texas but actually were from Mexico. They might have been in the United States illegally, but we never asked them.

I even had an opportunity sometimes to witness for the Christian faith. Some of them had gone to Sunday school at one time or other, but they didn't know much about the Bible or about the Lord.

Several times, in late summer, after the threshing season was over, Manny and I also worked with a sweet corn picking crew in the fields. The pay was $1.25 per ton, so each of the five in the crew got 25¢ of that.

We picked about sixteen tons every day (two big truck loads), so we each earned about $4, which wasn't too bad for working from daybreak to about two o'clock.

Also, one of those summers, I worked for a couple of weeks in the factory where they canned the corn on the border of South Dakota, between Ortonville, Minnesota, and Big Stone City, South Dakota.

One day, while working on a can-cooling crew at that corn-canning factory, I saw one of the boys take can after can out of the cooling crates, knock them on something, and throw them to the side. When I asked him what he was doing, he told me, "My mother told me to bring home a dozen cans of corn, and you know, we can only take the cans that are dented."

"What do you know," I thought, "that kid's a thief and probably doesn't realize it." I didn't say anything to him, though, because he was a pretty rough guy and much bigger than I was. I hoped maybe that my not doing the same thing would somehow be an example to him.

In 1948, after a summer session of education classes I attended in St. Paul, I worked in a pea-canning factory in Merrill, Wisconsin, for several weeks. The pay was only sixty cents an hour, but the worst part of that job was not the low pay. It was, rather, the monotony of the work. We had to take cans of peas from a conveyor belt and pack them into boxes. It was the same thing all day—every day.

Some women didn't mind doing that because they could do it without thinking while they jabbered to the others hour after hour, complaining about their husbands, their in-laws, or their children. To me, however, it was boring to do the same thing all day and hear those women constantly complain. Even their complaints didn't vary much!

The last week there, I was put on a labeling crew with a boss who was, shall we say, a little slow. He had to write down the simplest numbers to add up how many boxes were here or there. I swear he couldn't add five and five unless he wrote it down or counted on his fingers.

That fall, after working in the pea cannery, it was refreshing and very much more stimulating to go into a classroom to teach children. I wasn't tremendously prepared to teach, but I made it, as I've written about in one of the last chapters of this book. I mentioned there that I was *still growing up* both physically and mentally while I taught the first year in that one-room school.

I found out a few years later, that 1947 was the last summer those Western Minnesota farmers shocked grain and pitched grain bundles into threshing machines like they did in those years when I worked in those fields.

In 1948, most of them started to use combines. That's progress, I guess, but it must have changed things culturally for those farm families who did much of the harvesting work together.

It was good for me to earn something doing farm work. The pay wasn't that great, but the farm families were usually good people, and those folks ate well every day! That the meals were good was important to a growing boy.

I do still feel that farm work is best done by farmers and their families. They have a vested interest in what they do. I did appreciate it, though, that I had an opportunity to earn something during those summers. Also, meeting and working with so many different people was interesting.

When I heard, a few years later, that the farmers were all using combines to cut and thresh grain, I figured that I was born too soon.

CHAPTER THIRTY-TWO

JOURNEY TO STROMERS' IN 1939

In the fall of 1939, our parents decided to make a journey to the farm in Wisconsin where Dad first lived when he immigrated to the United States.

The four of us children who were still at home went along: Marty, who just turned thirteen; I, almost eleven; Manny, not quite nine; and Danny, who was a few months from five. We traveled in our '36 Chevy to Merrill, Wisconsin, about four hundred miles from our home in Odessa, Minnesota. Dad, of course, had to do all the driving, since Mom had never learned to drive, and the others of us were too young.

The first night at Stromers' was interesting. The room in which Manny and I slept had furniture and fixtures which seemed to be from the last century. In fact, there was a calendar on the wall that was almost thirty years old. Maybe Aunt Mary couldn't dispose of it because it had a pretty picture of a snowcapped mountain. It seemed as though she couldn't dispose of much of anything, no matter what little use it had.

There was nothing wrong with the house. It was the way the Stromers lived that seemed wrong to us, or at least quite different. The house was built by our father in 1910, the year before he left the farm to study for the ministry. He had told us all about that. He even boasted a little about how well it was built.

The Stromers lived *"behind the time"* ever since they had come from "the old country." They immigrated to America from Germany about 1890, and it seemed that they were still living in that time. *They were different,* to say the least.

After Mom and Dad spent some time with Aunt Mary, they went to bed. Aunt Mary Stromer sat for hours in the parlor, which was near the bedroom where we were. She was all alone, and she constantly babbled softly, except for a few outbursts. While Manny was sound asleep, I listened. I could tell that she was speaking in German, but I couldn't hear her well enough to understand much of what she was saying.

We left for home again after several days with Aunt Mary. For years after that, I wondered what Aunt Mary was saying as she sat there that night all by herself for hours.

When I was a senior in high school at Concordia in St. Paul, I wrote a story about that night for a creative writing segment of an English class.

I decided to include in this book a slightly revised version of the story I wrote when I was seventeen. The story is written as fiction, of course, because I couldn't make out much of what she was saying. However, everything in the story is consistent with the Stromers' life as I remember how it was told to us. Especially what is said about our father (Ihno) is what we were told by Dad many times in our youth. I've called the story, *"Tomorrow Will Be a Big Day."*

When you discover what the "Big Day" was, as you read the story, you will understand the reason for our trip. I am not telling you at this point what the big day was, because I want you to read the story first. I will write more about this experience and about the Stromers at the end of the story.

You may wonder what this has to do with growing up in the parsonage in Odessa. To understand the connection, you would have to know how many times the Stromers were spoken of in our home. They were the people who sponsored Dad in his immigration to America, and the experience Dad had with these "distant relatives" was indelible in his mind. I will say more about this after the story.

TOMORROW WILL BE A BIG DAY

(A fiction story, consistent with fact.)

The old woman sat almost motionless in a high-back rocker, staring toward where her husband lay. The only sounds heard in the room came from the ticking of the grandfather clock, the occasional rustling of the leaves outside the farmhouse, and the creaking of the rocker when its aged occupant made the slightest move.

The thin arms of the woman rested on the arms of the rocker, as her withered fingers tapped lightly, making almost no sound. She had been sitting there, as though in a trance for nearly an hour

Finally, she broke the silence with a weak sigh before she began to speak softly.

"Hattie and Herman said that you have to stay here in the parlor tonight, Hans, my dear." She leaned slightly forward and continued. "You will be all right, won't you, just for this one night? It's always a little chilly in here, even with a good fire in the kitchen."

Her eyes, barely open to a squint, were fixed on where her husband lay, as she seemed to wait for an answer. There was, however, no response. None at all. Her aged husband's eyes were shut, his mouth was closed, and his hands were still.

The year was 1939, but the room in which the woman sat looked like something out of the last century. The woman herself seemed to be a living anachronism, with her long, full skirt, high button shoes, and her cotton print bonnet, shading her face in the dim light.

"I hope you will sleep well, Hans, my dear. You need rest. Tomorrow will be a big day. Hattie said a lot of people will be here."

The face of the old woman, wrinkled with eighty-one years of hardship, broke into a slight smile, as she thought of "big day."

"Oh, Hans, do you remember the day in Stuttgard, when you and I promised not to part till death would part us? That was a big day too, wasn't it? Na ya, it sure

was." Her eyes closed and a tear dropped to her calico apron, as she thought about how long ago it was that they were married.

"Na ya, I'm sure you remember the day too, when you came from Berlin with the permission papers to go to America. Ya, that was a big day, too; no?" She paused. "At least it was for you." Again, tears welled up in her eyes. "I didn't tell you that day that we were finally going to be mama and papa. I . . . I didn't want to spoil the plans."

She shook her head in disbelief. "But things were not good. No, they were not good at all." Her head hung down, as she continued to see the past in her mind. "I'm so sorry. So sorry that our little one had to be put in that tiny coffin and lowered into the waves of the stormy sea, on our way to America."

Her eyes opened, and she stared, as though she was seeing the coffin float away. "If only the baby could have been baptized! But you said the Lord took him home, didn't you, Hans?" There was no response. "You know you did!" Her eyes closed again. "It was a son, Hans! A son! He could have helped us pull stumps here in Wisconsin! Na, ya, he could have been a big help to us here."

Raising her head slowly, she noticed a calendar on the wall near her, which was from 1907. But this was 1939! Then she remembered that she kept it because she liked the pretty picture of a covered bridge in Vermont.

Suddenly, the year 1907 triggered something in her mind. "Do you recall, Hans, my dear, what happened in

1907? Of course you do; that's when your nephew Ihno came from the old country." She shook her head slowly. "Ya, that was a big day too, but . . . but not for long."

Continuing to shake her head and wrinkling her forehead into a frown of disappointment, she went on. "He was to come to work with us, no? Yes, he was, but from day he arrived he talked about going to school!"

"Why should a young man want more book-learning? Hands are made for work, not for holding books, no? Na, ya, they are!" She opened her eyes in anger. "He was to be the son we never had! That's why we brought him here to be a son to help us, not to be a schoolboy."

The old woman, now full of frustration, wagged her head. "He would convince you, when a little snow fell, that it was too windy or too cold to work in the woods. Na ya, then he would run two miles through the wind and snow to the school in Pine River to study with the children! No, it was never too cold or windy to go to school!"

"He was some worker! Na ya, some worker he was! He had to go to school to learn English!" She shook her head more and grabbed the armrests of the chair like she was going to get up. "Why did he need to learn English? That's not what we speak, and that's not what farm folks here talk! Why did he need to learn English? Is that such a wonderful tongue?"

"Then, he wanted to go to church on Sunday, when you wanted him to help you in the woods. Na, ya, he couldn't even come to help on Sunday afternoon. He had to visit with the pastor's family—to practice more English with the pastor's daughter."

Raising her hands and shaking her head, she said, "What next?" She paused, then continued, "I'll tell you what next; he talked about studying for the ministry. What a foolish boy! What a very foolish boy!"

"The ministry?" I asked many times. "What money is there in the ministry?" "Oh," he said "you don't serve the Lord for money." "Na ya, I tried so hard to convince him that he should forget about the ministry."

Her eyes, which usually were no more than slits, now opened wide, as feelings of anger stirred her more. "What bothers me, Hans, is that he is still a fool today, after all these years! He still is!"

She sat back in the rocker, still shaking her head. "With a wife and all those children, he is still a fool! He really is! He will be here tomorrow with his preacher's-daughter wife and four or five of their brood."

"You will see, as you have in the past. They have nothing, but they act like they lack nothing! And the children have so little, but they act like they don't have a care in the world!" The old woman almost growled in a hoarse whisper, "Real fools, they are, Hans; you will see again tomorrow!"

With all this off her chest, the old woman slumped back into the chair once more. There she sat in silence for a few minutes, almost appearing to be paralyzed, staring toward her husband, as he lay motionless in front of her.

"We went on, though, didn't we, Hans, after Ihno went to that preacher school. We went on without the boy, and . . . and we cleared the land without him . . . by ourselves. Didn't we, Hans?" Again, her head hung down. "Maybe it was best for him to be a preacher . . . he was not a big boy, and his hands were small . . . too small to be a farmer . . . a real man of the soil." Seemingly finished with all she had to say, she sat staring straight ahead, not moving a muscle.

The silence was broken abruptly with a loud GONG of the grandfather clock! It broke the silence like a clap of thunder interrupts the sleep of the night! Actually, the clock was just calling out the half hour, but to her, it was as though she was being told that she should stop talking.

She opened her eyes and suddenly realized where she was and why she and her husband were there.

Laboriously, she got up out of the rocker and bent down over her husband and kissed his forehead. "Forgive me, Hans, for going on and on. Rest well now. Tomorrow will be a big day, like Hattie said."

The old woman stood for a moment over her husband's coffin, where he lay, dressed in his Sunday best. She touched his cold hands, as she whispered, "Sleep well, Hans; sleep well. Tomorrow will be a big day."

She straightened up her bent and withered body, the best she could, and turned around slowly. Then, with her hands folded into her apron, she shuffled slowly toward her bedroom.

THE END

A FOLLOW-UP

Uncle Stromer's body did, in fact, lie in state in a coffin in the parlor of their house the night before his funeral. Aunt Mary, when I heard her mumbling that night, was sitting, facing Uncle Stromer's coffin as she spoke. Imagining what she might be saying, and remembering what I had heard about their life gave me the idea for the story.

Several things are interesting about the Stromers' relationship with our father. Dad said that *the Stromers initiated his coming to America*. He did not *ask them* to help him get to America. Also, the Stromers knew that he was interested in studying to be an architect in the United States, but they told Dad's parents that they wanted Ihno, the youngest son in that family, to be the son they never had.

That meant that they wanted him to be with them on the farm, but they never told Dad that. They knew that he would come to America, if they offered to pay his way, because they knew that he wanted to leave Germany due to his dislike of the military aggressiveness of the Kaiser and others of the nation's leaders.

When he arrived in Wisconsin, however, in 1907, they treated him more like a servant than a son, even before he expressed the desire to study for the ministry. Dad said that he felt hurt when they required that he sleep in the haymow of the barn. Dad said that one time when he went to the house during a terrible thunderstorm in the night, Aunt Mary laughed at him and sent him back to the barn.

Even after Dad, a master carpenter, had built them a house almost singlehandedly in the summer of 1910, the Stromers publicly disowned him when he left the farm to begin his studies for the ministry.

Incidentally, Dad did not decide to study for the ministry after he got to know Pastor Theodore Thormaehlen and his daughter Minnie. It was, rather, the opposite; he became friends with the Thormaehlen family *after he decided to study for the ministry*. Stromers thought that Pastor Thormaehlen and his daughter Minnie persuaded Dad to study for the ministry. Not true.

He gave himself to the Lord and decided he wanted to serve Him *after he had a religious experience listening to a missionary from South America at a Lutheran mission festival in the woods not far from the Stromer's farm.*

It was a real blessing for Dad that the missionary preached in his native language—German. That religious experience prompted him to go to church the next Sunday where he met Pastor Thormaehlen and his family.

Although the Stromers had disowned Dad when he went to the seminary, Dad felt grateful to them for their helping him to get to America. He never disassociated himself from them. Whenever we traveled to Wisconsin, from Western Minnesota, we always spent two or three days with the Stromers, even though it was not really a pleasant experience for any of us.

When Aunt Mary could no longer live by herself several years after Uncle Stromer's death, our parents took Aunt Mary into their home near Merrill, Wisconsin, where they lived at the time. Mom and Dad took care of her for probably five years until her death in 1952. Aunt Mary was penniless and quite senile when Dad and Mom took her into their home to care for her.

At Aunt Mary's funeral, Dad spoke in a very Christlike way as he did also in 1939 at Uncle Stromer's funeral. Dad was more than a son to the Stromers, even though, in their minds, their nephew was a disappointment.

The Lord indeed works in mysterious ways to work out the plans He has for our lives. Father endured some very unhappy times in his first years here in America. Nonetheless, I do believe that God's will was done in his life, and regardless of the Stromers' thoughts toward him when he left their farm to study for the ministry, he was a blessing to them.

CHAPTER THIRTY-THREE

SNOWSTORMS ON THE PLAINS OF MINNESOTA

Where we lived when I was a child, there was plenty of snow most winters. In fact, the farmers in the area hoped and prayed that it would snow enough before there were hard freezes, especially if they had their fall plowing done.

The *blanket* of snow would keep the frost line in the ground from going down too far. Also, the moisture from the melted snow in the spring, especially on a field that had been plowed in fall, would give the land a head start for the growing season.

Snow is a good thing in many ways. We, as children growing up in Minnesota, thought it was wonderful! It was not only pretty, but it gave a covering to the hills, so we could ride down on our sleds. Also, snowdrifts sometimes were hard enough to walk on or even slide down if they were high enough. Snowbanks were hard especially after a blizzard with high winds. We kids thanked God for snow! We loved it!

We loved snowstorms, too! By snow*storm* I don't just mean *snowfall;* I mean when there was snow that was drier than usual (because of very cold air), blown by a high wind.

I've laughed at what is called a *snowstorm* in some places where I have lived, like here in Southern Arizona and even in the Philadelphia area, near the East Coast. People in those areas call *any snowfall* a storm. They don't really know what *a snowstorm* is. They especially do not realize what snowstorms are like at times on the plains of Western Minnesota or in any of the Northern Plains' states.

In the 1930s, sometimes a snowstorm *on those windswept plains* was so severe that almost everything stopped for days. That was called *a blizzard.*

The dictionary that I consulted just now says that a blizzard is a long severe snowstorm with high winds and fine snow. By *fine*, it means that the snow is almost like powder—containing the minimum of moisture.

We had snowstorms like that usually once or twice a winter. There were times when cattle and even the most hearty wildlife died. Of course, some *people* also froze to death in blizzards if they were lost or stranded. I remember storms in which cars, trucks, busses, and *even trains* were stranded in a blizzard, days at a time.

Today, even with different technology, from radios and phones to snow removal equipment, snowstorms are still dangerous in various ways. They certainly were worse, however, before that technology was developed.

Of course, weather is understood and predicted better today, which helps considerably. Also, there is much better high tech snow removal equipment, which is more scientifically operated.

In 1940, one of the worst snowstorms of the twentieth century in the United States hit the Midwest plains on Armistice Day (as Veterans' Day was called at that time). November 11 that year was on Monday, so many people who traveled over the long weekend were returning that day.

That blizzard was extremely dangerous because of the amount of snow, the sustained high winds, and below zero temperatures which continued for days. Even pheasants in the wild, and domestic turkeys grown for Thanksgiving were frozen by the thousands.

The worst, however, was the stranding of cars, trucks, buses, and even trains. So many people died! Some vehicles, in fact, which were abandoned by people who got stuck in the snow, were not found until the snow melted *in spring*!

Most of the teachers in Odessa were single women, so they had gone home for that long Armistice Day weekend in 1940. They didn't get back for more than a week because the blizzard lasted for several days, and many roads were closed due to the high, hard drifts. Also, as I have indicated, snow removal equipment was not what it is today.

A big storm like that seemed nice for us kids at the time. We didn't have school that whole week! It wasn't so nice, however, to have a shorter Christmas vacation in December, so that those lost days could be made up.

During the days of that severe November blizzard, it was not possible to go anywhere. In fact, when the storm was raging at its worst, we even had problems getting out to the shed to get wood and coal for our stoves.

Dad and Vernon (the oldest at home at the time) tied a rope between the house and the shed so that day or night, we could find the shed where our fuel was—firewood, coal, kindling, and corncobs.

We ate whatever we had since we were not able to get to the store or to the farm on the edge of town where we got our milk. We had no refrigerator, but fortunately, we had a lot of canned goods, potatoes, sauerkraut, and flour to make bread.

Our only "refrigerator" was the back porch, but we had to be careful what we put out there because it was more like a freezer—very cold most of the time. Things froze out there rather quickly.

It was difficult also to keep the outside water pump from freezing up. That pump, fortunately, was no more than about thirty feet from our back porch. Someone had to go out to the pump every few hours to pump some water to try to keep it from freezing solid down in the well.

The big square, box parsonage in which we lived was not weatherproofed. Fortunately, in October, we had put a "blanket" of tarpaper around the base of the house, extending about three feet up from the ground, attached with laths. Then we shoveled snow against that.

It helped some to keep the cold wind out during that terrible storm.

The wind whistled around and *sometimes even through* our house, but we managed to keep warm enough with fires in the stoves, extra blankets on the beds, and heavy clothes on ourselves even while we were in the house.

During the big storms, like the one in November of 1940, after we got our *chores* done each day, we kids had a wonderful time putting together jigsaw puzzles and playing games of all kinds.

Our favorite game, rather new at that time, was *Monopoly*; Sometimes we kept a Monopoly game going *for several days*. We made up special *depression rules*, which included borrowing from the bank and putting money from "fines" and "penalties" on "Free Parking."

I remember that little Danny Bill, only six years old, learned a lot of arithmetic by playing Monopoly with us, especially with our special rules.

There was, of course, no television at that time, but we did have radio and listened intently, especially to news broadcasts and weather reports. We even had shortwave radio on which Dad listened to the news every day.

If a blizzard lasted for days, like the one did in November of 1940, our folks also had us work on school lessons if we had books and materials with us at home.

I wasn't smarter than my brothers and sisters, but I must have used my time better in school, or something, because I rarely brought homework home from school. I usually got my work done at school, so I rarely had any schoolwork to do at home. Mom and Dad encouraged me to help Manny.

Also, to give me something to do during a blizzard when the others were working on their lessons, Dad would sometimes try to teach me Latin. He thought this would help me if I would study for the ministry later.

The problem was that he only knew how to explain the Latin grammar rules *in German,* and he was more comfortable translating the Latin paragraphs into German rather than English.

My knowledge of German wasn't that great, but I learned more of the language at those times. In a way then, I was learning something of both Latin and German. I remember that I sometimes got the languages mixed up, but at least I was learning.

I wish Dad would have just taught me more German and German grammar. A few years later, when I studied German at prep school, I got along in German conversation better than some of my classmates but lacked an understanding of the grammar of the language.

During a real severe blizzard, like the one in 1940, sometimes the wind would howl around the house, something awful! It sounded sometimes like we were going to be blown off the face of the earth!

When the snow and wind were very bad, especially at night, Dad got us together for special devotions and prayers like he often did during severe summer thunderstorms. That was a great comfort.

Dad and Mom believed fervently that God had all things in His hands and they really carried through with what they believed. Their confidence in the Lord was contagious.

After that snowstorm in 1940, there were snowdrifts in places as high as the roofs on barns and houses. We kids had a lot of fun climbing up and sliding down the drifts. It was extremely difficult, however, for snowplows to clear the roads and streets in order for people to get around with vehicles.

Because snow removal equipment wasn't what it is today, many of those snowdrifts could not be removed too easily, even with big snowplows.

Some of the snowdrifts did not melt away until late spring. Nineteen forty was a winter people will never forget! And to think that the Armistice Day snowstorm occurred *in November*! Technically, that was *before winter began!*

If you've ever read the *Little House on the Prairie* books by Laura Ingels Wilder, you remember her story called *the Long Winter*. From that, you get an idea of what we experienced on the plains of Western Minnesota in winter of 1940 to '41.

The Ingels family, of course, had it worse than we did because that was in the 1880s. The technology in 1940 wasn't that great, but it was a lot better than what they had in the nineteenth century.

The area, incidentally, which Laura Ingels Wilder was writing about in *the Long Winter* (in southeast South Dakota) was not ~~too~~ that far from where we lived in Minnesota, maybe one hundred fifty miles.

That 1940 November snowstorm has been said to have been the worst of the century, but it was *one of many* we had. They weren't all as bad as that one, of course, but storms *half that bad* were still dangerous.

When we were children; however, snowstorms were always *fun,* in a way. Anytime we heard Mom answer the telephone about seven thirty in the morning and then call upstairs and say, "No school today!" we'd get dressed faster than usual! That usually happened several times each winter.

Sometimes the storm wasn't so bad that those of us who lived in the village couldn't get to school, but it was dangerous to make lengthy bus trips out in the country to get the students in from the farms. School days were very different, if only the students in town could get to school.

If there was a snowfall of several inches during the school day, especially if it was cold and the snow was drier than usual, they'd bring the buses to the school in the middle of the day and take home the children who lived in rural areas. The school superintendent knew that if a wind would start up, when there was several inches of powdery snow on the ground, *there would be a storm.*

It's not that easy to remember everything about those snowstorms in Minnesota which we experienced years ago, especially since I'm a lot older now and have lived and worked in Arizona for nearly fifty years.

There are times, however, when my imagination makes those days seem like yesterday. In fact, while writing this chapter, I had to put a long-sleeved shirt on, although it's a pleasant October day here in Southern Arizona, *because I felt cold just thinking about it*!

When I was working as pastor of Lutheran students at the University of Arizona in the early 1960s, I told them in December that it didn't seem like Christmas to me without snow. A girl from Yuma, Arizona, who had never seen snow at Christmastime, said, "How much snow did the shepherds trudge through on their way to Bethlehem?"

I had to admit—that was something to think about. Indeed, what does snow have to do with Christmas? It's all in our minds, depending on our experience.

As I said, snow and even snowstorms were fun for us as children. Today, at my age, it's a little different. When our son Ted was about five (while we lived in Douglas, Arizona), he said one winter day that he was praying for snow. (We did have a little snow there once in a while, because of the nearly five thousand-foot elevation.)

I told our son that although snow was beautiful on trees and fun for children, it was dangerous for people traveling on the highways. A little later, he told me that he had changed his prayer. *He was praying that there would only be snow in the yards, not on the roads.* There's a thought!

I did not come to Arizona to get away from the winter weather in Minnesota, but I'm sure it would take a lot to persuade me to go back.

My wife, who was brought up in Mexico, had never seen a lake frozen over until she traveled to Minnesota and Wisconsin a few years ago. (*I like to tell people that she always wanted to walk on water, and ice was her only chance.*) Just kidding.

After a two-week trip to Minnesota and Wisconsin in winter and ample opportunity to walk on a frozen lake, she has talked about how beautiful it was. She is, however, happy to be back in sunny Arizona.

I still love to see snow today—*on Rincon Mountain Peak*, visible from our front door here near Benson, Arizona, forty miles from Tucson—and *on calendars and Christmas cards!* As much as I loved snow when I was a child, today, after all these years, *the memory of snow is enough.*

CHAPTER THIRTY-FOUR

BASEBALL IN ODESSA DURING WORLD WAR II

In the 1930s there were good baseball teams in all the small towns in our part of the country—Western Minnesota and eastern South Dakota. Games were played with pretty good crowds watching and cheering every Sunday afternoon all summer long.

The players were young men from all walks of life who were quite skilled at playing the game. That changed to some degree in the early to midforties. There weren't many able-bodied young men around; almost all them were in the service of our country, or they had migrated to cities as far away as California to work in war plants.

Consequently, the baseball players were boys who were too young for military service, men who *had at one time been better players* or farmers' sons deferred from military service for work on the farm.

We had a baseball team in Odessa during the war. We had a lot of fun and won some games, but most of us weren't that especially skilled at playing the game. What could you expect from the young and inexperienced, the men whose glory days of baseball were past, or farm boys who were tired on Sundays from doing dawn-to-dusk hard farm work all week?

When I say we weren't the best, or that we weren't like the players in previous years, I don't mean there weren't some good games. The teams were much the same in other towns, so teams were fairly equal. Competition was good, and we enjoyed playing on Sunday afternoons.

When I say that we weren't the greatest, I don't want you to think that we were like the kid in a tee ball league. Maybe you've heard about the young boy who hit a ball that was fumbled by several players, so he kept on running. When this little boy was rounding third base, members of his team yelled, "Go home, Joey! Go home, Joey!" So he turned sharply and ran across the street to his house.

No, I'm happy to say that we weren't anything like that. I do remember a farm boy, though, who was a nice guy but not the greatest shortstop. It seemed he could have his legs positioned right and his mitt right there; still the ball would get through there somehow.

What was interesting was that when this fellow would miss two or three in a row, he'd call to me on the pitcher's mound, shouting, "Come on, Arlo, settle down, and get these guys out," as though he had nothing to do with the bases being loaded with only one hit!

Of course, I wasn't the greatest pitcher either. One time, when we were playing in a little town in eastern

South Dakota, our coach said to me, "Keep 'em high and inside. I know these guys; they can't hit 'em there."

Well, my control wasn't always that good. I pitched *high and outside rather than high and inside*. What do you know? The first four batters hit homeruns.

When the coach started out to the mound, I thought he was going to give me "*what for,*" with some words I heard Dad say many times but only in a theological sense.

Instead, he stood in front of me, put his hands on his hips, kicked some dirt, and mumbled without looking up at me, "Well, at least you got the cleanup guy out of there, lettin' him knock in only one run!" He paused, kicked some more dirt, as he said in a rough but soft voice, still not looking up at me, "So settle down now, will ya? Yer really the only pitcher we got with us today, and you've only thrown about eight pitches so far! Come on, let's go after these guys!"

The way he viewed the situation was unbelievable! After all our players found out what he said, they laughed, hung loose, and played hard enough that we won that game ten to nine in ten innings!

Speaking of my pitching, one time I wound up to pitch and leaned back so far that I fell over backwards. Naturally, I got razzed something awful by the people in Correll where we were playing that day.

Two "cowboys" who were watching the game while sitting on their horses near the bleachers turned the horses around when I fell over. I guess they wanted to show me the part of the horse they thought I most resembled at that moment.

Another time, when some of the members of my family had come to see me pitch in Clinton, north of Ortonville, I hit three batters with pitched balls in the first inning. Fortunately, I didn't throw the ball ninety miles an hour, like the pros do today. In fact, the speed limit on the highways during the war was only thirty-five miles per hour, and I didn't break the speed law too much with my pitching.

Nonetheless, after hitting three of their players, the Clinton people wanted to kill me. One of my brothers-in-law even thought *his* life was in danger because they had heard him cheer for me.

That time, the coach took me off the mound and sent me to right field. Later in the game, I ran after a foul ball off the right field line and ran smack into an old popcorn stand!

Although it probably looked like I had killed myself crashing into that shed, the Clinton fans cheered! I guess they all felt better after that as though things had been kind of evened up. Fortunately, I wasn't really badly injured, except for my pride, but I guess it did the Clinton people some good to think I was.

A part of one summer, when it was too muddy to play on the town square in Odessa, we played several games in a pasture on higher ground near Highway 75 where a baseball diamond had been set up.

The infield was always cleaned out pretty well of *cow pies and other delicacies,* but the outfield wasn't. If a fielder slipped and fell while chasing a fly ball, everybody cheered heartily, knowing pretty sure why he fell. It added to the excitement, in a way, I guess. As I said, we did have fun, and we won some games.

We had an interesting player who had seen better days and was carrying forty pounds extra that he'd gotten from emptying a lot of Grain Belt draft into his gullet. The guy could, however, hit a ball a mile, if he didn't strike out.

We always said *he had to hit the ball over the fence*; that way he could run as slowly as his beer belly would let him. Otherwise, he wouldn't make it around the bases.

Thinking of the teams all being similarly mediocre during the war, when most of the better players were in the military, I heard the best one about a game at that time. I heard that this took place somewhere in Minnesota.

The first baseman on this team was injured in some way, so for the last out of the game, they put a man at first who had usually played third base.

The next batter missed on the third strike, and the ball hit the dirt, almost gotten by the catcher. As the batter ran toward first base, the catcher threw the ball to the first baseman and followed the batter. The man playing first, who was accustomed to playing third base, threw the ball back to the catcher.

Amazingly, *they got the batter in the "hotbox," between first and home!* Everyone was confused—even the batter who ran back and forth between the catcher and the first baseman. Finally, the catcher dropped the ball, and the batter dived into home base—safe!

Honest, folks, I heard that, but I can't believe either that it really happened. If it did, I think it must have occurred in a suburb of Wobegon, Minnesota, where the girls may be pretty, but some of the boys are below average in the skills of America's pastime.

Before I wind up this sports highlight chapter, I have to tell you something that is the gospel truth. One summer, we organized a game at the end of the season in Odessa between the younger guys and the players who *were more or less "over the hill."* We played the game for a case of beer, just for the fun of it.

In a close game, we younger guys won, so we got the beer. We took it over to the parsonage nearby. It was a good thing my father, who was pastor of most of the team members, was not back yet from his afternoon service at the rural church he served.

A whole gang of guys and some girls came over to the parsonage yard to share *the booty.* With almost as many people as there are bottles of beer in a case, there wasn't going to be any intoxicating going on. We just had fun! I think some of the beer was even poured out on Dad's morning glories in our backyard.

Something did however happen to me because of that experience. When my coach at Concordia in St. Paul found out that I had played for a case of beer, I was judged ineligible for the school team at Concordia.

Now, here's the unbelievable part. When I approached the coach about it, I was told that it was not only because I played baseball *for beer,* but because *the beer was considered pay!* He said I was no longer an amateur.

I guess you could say that my school days of baseball ended *when I turned pro.*

Oh well, on the school team at Concordia I had spent most of the time warming the bench, anyway. So after that, I just sat on the bench during the games *without a baseball suit on.*

CHAPTER THIRTY-FIVE

MY JOB AS CHURCH JANITOR

In January of 1942, when I was going on fourteen, I was employed as janitor of Trinity Lutheran Church. The church was next door to the parsonage in which we lived.

There was *no euphemism* for my job, not even *custodian*; I was *the janitor*. The pay was $50 for the year. The trustees who hired me said if I did a good job, I'd receive $2 extra at Christmas time, to make it an even dollar a week for the fifty-two weeks of the year.

The job required that I clean the church and the little church school, start furnace fires, mow the lawn in the summer, shovel snow in winter, and ring the bells.

I never told Dad that I prayed that the snow would not accumulate too much on the church steps or the sidewalk, especially on Saturday night or Sunday morning.

I thought the Lord would have a little mercy on me that way. Sometimes it seemed like my prayers were answered in the affirmative, but there were times too when it seemed as though I was tested. The snow was pretty deep.

I loved ringing the bells; I think *I'd have paid them* to let me ring those bells. It was a joy, but not easy *to do right*. There were two large bells, and they didn't simply go, *ding dong, ding dong*. The ratio was two to three, so it went more like *ding dong ding, ding dong ding*. Folks said it sounded like it was saying, "Come to church, come to church," when it was done right.

Grandpa Arndt, who lived a few blocks up the hill from the church, was the *master bell ringer*. He'd done it, I think for fifty years, and he was really good at it even in his old age.

He taught me how to do it, and Manny and I learned just when to hang on the ropes to slow them down or stop them at the right time.

The bells had to be rung at six Saturday evening, an hour before services on Sunday morning, at church time, the day someone died, and at the time of the funeral.

After a funeral service, the bell was *tolled* while the procession went to the cemetery to announce the age of the person who had died. No one, not even women, I guess, minded having their age revealed at the time of their funeral. After all, they had already gone to be with the Lord, so they weren't here to hear it.

The first time I rang the bells for a funeral, interestingly it was for Grandpa Arndt's; he was over ninety years old. I thought of that dear old man with every sound of the bells. In fact, when I tolled the bell while the procession was on the way to the cemetery for his burial, I cried all by myself up there in the bell tower. I couldn't help thinking of what a wonderful man he was and how patient he was in teaching me to ring those bells.

There were other times too when I thought it was so sad to toll the bell—especially when the bell was tolled only a few times, to indicate that it was *a young child who had died.*

A few years ago, when I visited the cemetery to pause for prayer at our brother Waldemar's grave, *I noticed how many tiny graves there were in that cemetery.* Some I remembered as the children who went to be with the Lord at the time that I was ringing the bells. It seems that it was much more common for young children to die at that time.

One problem with the bell ringing was that the bells had to be rung at *six on the dot on Saturday evening*; we found out that some people *set their clocks by it.*

There were times when I had to run home fast from my paper route to ring the bells at six on Saturday. There were other times too when it was hard to make it at the exact time, but I always tried my best so people wouldn't set their clocks wrong or think I wasn't doing my job right.

Also, I'd sometimes have to be released from school to ring the bells for a funeral. I got called the *Bim-Bam Boy* by my cousin, Junior Mews, because of that. (Bim-bam *pronounced as "bim bomb"*—was what a bell *"said"* in German.)

The lawn was not easy to mow (we had only a large old reel-type push mower), but Manny and Danny sometimes helped if I bought them a bottle of pop. In the real tough places, I pushed, and Manny and Danny pulled in front with ropes we tied to the mower.

While we mowed, I sometimes acted like I was plowing a field with a hand plow and a team. I was going to say, "*a team of mules,*" but Manny and Danny didn't like it when I called out, "Ya, ya, let's get goin' there!" 'cuz they knew what I was thinking.

It was especially hard to mow around the many flowerbeds that Dad and some of the women of the church had put in to beautify the church grounds. The hardest was around where Dad had made a rock garden, spelling TRINITY on the road side of the church. The moss roses were pretty, though, each morning in the summer. It was just hard to mow around all those rocks.

What I liked the least was *cleaning*. The church always looked bigger when it had to be cleaned. Also, the little church school had to be cleaned every week for Saturday confirmation classes and for Sunday school.

Also, the outhouse (attached to the woodshed) had to be cleaned every week. Most of the time, that wasn't too much of a problem, unless it was used by hobos when they came to the parsonage for a handout. Although my folks always fed those guys, they weren't too tidy about things.

Cleaning the church itself was the hardest. Everything, including all the pews, had to be dusted, and the floors (all hardwood) had to be cleaned with a dust mop every week and mopped once a month. It all had to be done also in the balcony.

It was nice when Marcia would help me. I let her use my bike to go riding with her boyfriend, so she was quite willing to help me with the cleaning. She was really better at cleaning than I was. I guess girls are always better at things like that—at least, more conscientious, for sure. Anyway, I always appreciated Marty's help. She was a very helpful sister—more like a good friend.

There was another thing I did to show my appreciation to Marcia. She was a cheerleader, so she was supposed to go to all the high school basketball games. I went along with her *as a chaperone*. (That's what Dad called it.)

Of course, *I never told anybody* that I was supposed to be Marty's *chaperone*. I just went along to the games, too, and didn't keep that much of *an eye on her* like Dad thought I did.

I always sat in a different part of the bus and didn't keep her from sitting with her boyfriend; that, she appreciated. Also, when we came home after the trips to those games, I'd wait for Marty on the church steps while she and her boyfriend *"said good night"* behind a tree at the corner of the church.

She helped me clean the church sometimes too, partly because *just the two of us were there to talk to each other*. At times like that she'd tell me everything that was on her mind. Marty could dust or mop and talk at the same time and never miss a beat. That was good. I appreciated it that *she didn't have to stop to talk.*

I couldn't advise her much; I just listened, not being *a matchmaker* or anything like that, and I didn't know much of anything about boy-girl stuff. I just tried to be a good "friend." It was always good to have her help no matter how much she talked or what she talked about.

When I had no help with the church cleaning, it took longer, of course, but it was actually good to be alone in God's house at times. I knew that God was everywhere, *but in His house, it was like I was alone with Him.* That made the cleaning a little more worthwhile.

Sometimes I would sit still in a pew and pray for a few minutes or kneel at the altar all by myself. Also, at times I'd step into the pulpit and say a few words that I'd heard Dad say the Sunday before. Of course, I never did that when there was someone with me.

While in the pulpit, I wondered if I'd ever be standing there to actually preach about the love of Jesus *as the pastor of a congregation.* I sure hoped so, but that seemed like it would be *a long way down the road,* if ever.

I thought maybe the *Second Coming of Christ* would occur before I would become a pastor. In the meantime, in December of 1942 when we again celebrated *His First Coming,* I got paid the fifty dollars for the year, and *I got the extra two dollars!*

The elders said I had earned it; that was nice to hear, and the two dollars came in handy, along with the fifty, at Christmas time. For one thing, I bought gifts for the family, especially for my helpers.

CHAPTER THIRTY-SIX

OUR MOTHER, A GIFT FROM GOD FOR US AND FOR DAD

Much has been said in this book about *my pastor father*. As I've read all the preceding chapters again, I've thought that not enough was said about *my mother*. She was very important to me as well as to all my brothers and sisters and all who knew her.

In addition to her being our loving mother, she was Dad's closest friend and companion. In fact, I would regard her as an integral part of Dad's ministry. I do not mean that she directed him or was domineering; *she was rather a real help to him—his best friend and personal confidant.*

Mother was a pastor's daughter. As the oldest of seven children in the family of the Reverend and Mrs. Theodore Thormaehlen, she may have learned more about being a pastor's wife than some of the others in that family. No one will ever know that, I guess, because she was the only one of the five daughters who married a pastor.

She, however, did not seek out a pastor to marry, nor did she encourage our father to become a pastor. Not at all! It seems rather that *she married Ihno Janssen who happened to be a pastor, not because he was a pastor.*

No one in our family, other than our father, ever knew Mom's mother. She died in childbirth when our Uncle Walter, mother's youngest brother was born. That occurred in January of 1917, six months after Mom and Dad were married (July 5, 1916).

We sometimes joked that Uncle Walter was on Dad and Mother's wedding picture with the family; *Grandma Thormaehlen was about three months pregnant with Walter in July of 1916 when that picture was taken.*

Sister Ruth was born in April of 1917, three months after Grandma died. Ruth and Uncle Walter more or less grew up together much like brother and sister; Walter spent part of his growing up years with our family and graduated from high school in Odessa ('34).

I have a feeling that our mother's mother (grandma Thormaehlen) was a warm, loving person because *our mother, her oldest daughter, certainly was.* Aunt Betty Moellendorf, the sister of mother's with whom I have had the most contact, remembers her mother as very personal and loving; however, Tabea (Aunt Betty) was just a child when her mother died in 1917.

Our mother's pastor father was an intellectual as well as a dedicated theologian and Bible scholar. However, he quite evidently did not have a warm personality. That's what I heard, especially from Aunt Betty and Uncle Walter as well as from Uncle George Moellendorf, Aunt

Betty's husband, who knew his father-in-law, Grandpa Thormaehlen, well.

The oldest two in our family, Ihno and Ruth, agreed with that. Ruth and Ihno Junior were twenty-two and twenty-one when Grandpa Thormaehlen died in 1939. Consequently, they knew Grandpa better than any others in the family.

Both Ruth and Ihno also remember Grandpa pretty well *from the first year our family was in Odessa (1927).* At that time Grandpa was still the pastor of Immanuel Lutheran Church in Yellow Bank. (He retired in January of 1928, about a year after our family moved to Odessa.)

I don't recall that our mother ever said much about her father. In fact, *our dad said more.* He admired his father-in-law Pastor Thormaehlen for his intelligence and intellectuality as well as for his being a good theologian. However, Dad was adversely critical of Grandpa's moodiness and being withdrawn—sometimes appearing aloof.

When anyone in our family, as we were growing up, would *pout or act sullen,* Dad was quick to react, in an effort to rectify the situation even if it involved any of us as young children. It seemed that Dad feared that we might be displaying a proclivity toward traits inherited from Grandpa Thormaehlen—traits that Dad thought were a disadvantage in life.

Our father liked to see signs of intelligence and studiousness in us children such as they were to be found. However, he disliked any moodiness and hoped it could be prevented or *nipped in the bud.*

Our mother was a very loving person, but a good disciplinarian. We always thought it was ironic that *she said she didn't like disciplining children when she taught school.* We had a hard time understanding that because we knew her as a person who could so skillfully use *the iron hand in a velvet glove* in dealing with all of us children. Actually, she rarely used her hand for discipline; *a look was usually enough.*

Mother's father went to be with the Lord in 1939, when I was just eleven, and Grandpa lived in Wisconsin the last ten years of his life, four hundred miles from us. Consequently, I do not remember much about him. He rarely came to visit us.

I do know that he was with us in Odessa and preached for our father on Christmas Eve at Trinity in Odessa, just a few months before he died. It was a good sermon; I even recall some of the things he said, though I was only ten at Christmastime in 1938.

Mom had studied music and was an accomplished pianist and church organist. She played for worship services at Trinity in Odessa for many years. She also played for services in Yellow Bank almost every Sunday even though she had her hands full with so many children at home.

The church organs at that time were the old type, the air pumped with foot pedals. Occasionally, a pedal strap broke, at which time one of us kids would have to run up to the organ and pump with a handle in the back of the organ. It's amazing how she could get our attention fast enough to get one of us there so that she hardly missed a beat in the liturgy or a hymn. She was a good organist and knew how to handle problems with the organ.

All her organ playing, both in Odessa and in Yellow Bank, was volunteer work—just done, I suppose, as a part of Dad's ministry. The congregations would sometimes give her a few dollars at Christmastime, but only as a gift. Mom also taught our sister Ruth to play, and she became a good musician too.

For years, Mom also directed the choir in Odessa, especially in the Christmas and Easter seasons. Almost always there was one or more of our family in her choir. We were all musically inclined and did a lot of singing in the family. Dad, who also was a fairly good musician, often played the piano and sang with us.

I sang in Mom's choir when I was younger than the others. I could sing soprano, alto, and later, tenor. Where she had me sing depended on where the need was the greatest. Mom appreciated that and made the most of it. She even had me as part of the choir, sing a solo once in a while.

When I was a teenager, my voice hadn't changed that much; I could still sing alto—where Mom usually needed me most. I would sing alto when she wanted me to *if she would let me stand with the men, not the women.*

She granted my wish, I'm sure, *because it was good for the choir.* She surely did not give in to me *because I was her son.* When any of us from the family were in the church choir, it was as though she was not our mother; *she was the choir director.* We always respected that.

Singing with the women in the choir Mom directed while standing with the men helped me to feel the musical harmony in a special way.

Years later, when I sang in the Concordia Seminary Chorus at Springfield, Illinois, I always asked the director to place me in the middle of the chorus even when there were more than seventy in the group *so that I could feel all the harmony*. My request was always granted when I explained to the director that I wanted to be able to hear all parts.

Also, I suppose Mom's training helped me to be the leader of a semiprofessional quartette I sang with during my seminary years. Although I was not a pianist, I'm sure that I succeeded as the leader mostly because I'd learned something about *leadership in music* from my mother. I was *not the lead singer* in the quartette, by the way, *just the leader of the group.*

Another way in which Mom was a blessing to all of us was that she guided and directed us; in fact, she never gave up on us, no matter what happened. I'll use the example of brother Vernon who I'm sure wasn't the easiest to rear as a child. He had ability, but at times was obstinate. Regardless, he was loved just as all of us were and was given positive direction.

Vernon aggravated Dad quite frequently. Why, I don't know, probably because Dad made too many comparisons between Ihno and Vernon. That certainly didn't do Vernon any good because Ihno and Vernon were very different—in personality and ability. Although Vernon didn't always do as well in school as Mom and Dad wanted him to and frequently ruffled the feathers of teachers, Mom never "gave up" on him. Rather, she encouraged him in every way she could.

I'm not sure how much Vernon appreciated Mom's encouragement *until he went into the army at nineteen in 1943.*

While in the service, Vernon wrote home almost every day even when he was overseas *"in the thick of it"* during World War II. His letters, I know, showed his love for our parents, especially for our mother.

To be sure, Mother wrote back to Vernon at least two or three times a week, and she got our dad involved too. She also quite regularly encouraged us kids to write to Vern.

I know that the letters from home meant a lot to Vernon. It was obvious that he thought a lot about home, our family, and the Christian faith while he was serving our country.

After he returned from the war, there was no one in the family any closer to our parents than Vernon. Also, he was a very committed Christian, very much involved in the Lord's work, even assisting pastors wherever he lived.

Also, after Vernon's return from the war, when he and his wife Phyllis lived in Minneapolis, he was a very thoughtful brother to Manny and me while we were at prep school in St. Paul. He was of help to us in so many ways.

It is my opinion that Mother's constant encouragement had much to do with Vernon's coming closer to the Lord and to the family as well as doing well in his life's work.

Incidentally, I would love to have the letters Vernon wrote home during the war and the letters our folks and we siblings wrote to him. I'm sure that correspondence would make an interesting book on family relationships, but the letters have been lost over the years, probably when the folks moved to Wisconsin in 1947.

Our mother was also exceptional in the kitchen, not so much in her ability to cook or bake, but in her ability *to make whatever we had tasty* and her special ability to *stretch the food to feed all of us adequately.*

When we prayed together around the table, *Kom, Herr Jesu, sei unser Gast, und segne was Du uns beschert hast* (Come, Lord Jesus, be our Guest, and bless what You have given us), *we truly felt blessed with whatever we had and were especially thankful that the Lord Jesus was always present with us.* Mom's loving hands and God's presence were more important than having great quantity or magnificent quality!

Mom was also *the most hospitable woman you could find anywhere.* No matter how many of our family were around the table, there was always room for another one. That was true also of staying the night, or longer. We so frequently had others staying with us during a snowstorm or any time there was a need. In fact, in 1938, when we were all still home, Ihno brought a roommate home to stay the entire summer.

I don't remember our mother complaining when any of us brought friends home with us. That was especially true when we were in prep school or college. Roommates or friends were always welcome. At that time, phones were not what they are today, so it was not uncommon for friends to be brought home unannounced.

Of course, a penny postcard sometimes announced forthcoming events to us and for that matter, sometimes to the whole town. I remember one morning when I came to the post office, the postmaster said, "I'll bet you're happy that your brother and a roommate are coming this weekend." When I registered surprise, he said nervously, "I don't remember who told me that."

Actually, *the all-noticing postmaster* had read the mail already that morning. After hearing what the postmaster said, I found in our PO box the card announcing Ihno's coming home with a roommate.

In another chapter of this book, I mention that the *Cotton Blossom Singers* from a black school in Mississippi came to sing at our church. When my parents, especially our mother, saw how cramped the quarters were in the *"house bus,"* in which they lived, those men were invited to stay with us in our house. They were also invited to eat with us whenever they were in our area at mealtime.

That kind of hospitality, I'm happy to say, was about the same in most of the families of my brothers and sisters. My sister Marcia, the last of the sisters, is a prime example of the hospitality learned from our mother. Everyone is always welcome at Marty's house.

Though our mother was a strikingly pretty woman in her younger years, she was a little overweight after bearing ten children. She always was conscious of her weight and frequently tried to do something about it.

What woman wouldn't have gained weight after ten pregnancies? Imagine enduring *ninety months of pregnancy*! Dad sometimes joked that *his wife weighed ninety pounds when he married her, and it was a double-or-nothing gamble, and he won.*

That reminds me—Mom played basketball when she attended a teachers college in Wisconsin in her late teens. Dad carried in his wallet, believe it or not, *a picture of Mom in a girls' basketball uniform*. The girls "suited up" quite differently in 1912, '13, and '14; nonetheless, it was a sport uniform she had on, and she was a pretty girl and very trim at the time.

Dad liked to show that picture to people, just for the fun of it—not at all, I'm happy to say, to ridicule her. I was with him one time in Merrill, Wisconsin, when *he showed that photo of Mother in a basketball uniform to a policeman who asked him for his driver's license.*

Dad said to the policeman as he showed him the picture of Mom in her teens, "Here is a picture of my wife just before we got married." I think the cop thought Dad, in his sixties at the time, was a little flaky, so he let him go. That cop had no sense of humor, but it did save Dad a little money. Maybe that's why he showed him the picture and spoke the way he did.

Mom's sister Clara and her family lived in Odessa for years. Several times when I was with young Erich at Aunt Clara Mews' house, she said something like this about our mother, *"Poor Min, with all those children!"* I thought to myself, *"Poor Aunt Clara, with only one child!* What fun is that?"

Incidentally, *where do you think that one child of hers (Erich Junior) was most of the time?* At our house, of course, *with poor Aunt Minnie and all those children!*

Mom was a very good mother who knew how to command our respect and love with virtually no violence. As I've said, a look of dissatisfaction from her, when we were out of line, was more effective than a spanking.

No matter how busy Mother was, she always took time to sing and pray with us at bedtime. To this day, when I pray upon going to bed, I think of our wonderful Christian mother, and I frequently recall the songs we sang together in both German and English. I even remember most of the words of all those songs, even the ones in German.

Abraham Lincoln said that *all he was, he owed to his mother*. We in our family, likewise, owed so much to our mother in so many ways. Everyone in our family knew that and appreciated it.

In addition to her meaning so much to us, she was a wonderful friend and confidante for our pastor father. *I don't think she ever told him what to do,* but she listened to him, no matter how happy or frustrated he might have been at times.

I remember many times when she would leave what she was doing in the kitchen and *go to his study for a talk* when he asked her to. And at the end of the day, in the church and parsonage yard in Odessa and later on Snow Hill where they lived near Merrill, Wisconsin, they frequently took walks together on a summer evening. They seemed to enjoy walking and talking quietly, just the two of them.

Mom was a great help to our pastor father, and there were ways in which Dad was of help to Mother in her work too. He didn't help much in the kitchen (I don't think he could boil water), but he helped make beds and clean the house; also, *he took his day off almost every week to help Mom with washing clothes.*

I don't know what Dad would have done without her in his ministry, as well as in his life. When Dad proposed to Mom when they were in their twenties, he may have said, *"You mean everything to me!"* At that time, I'm sure he didn't know how much she would mean to him in his ministry and in their nearly fifty years of marriage.

When she went to be with the Lord in 1961, several years before Dad died, he did have to go on with his life and even with his ministry in a small rural congregation in Wisconsin. *It was evident, however, that he missed her very much and yearned to be with her again.*

Dad preached the night he died. It was in a Lenten service just a few weeks before *the Festival of the Resurrection in 1964.* At Dad's funeral, a member of his church said to me about Dad's preaching the night he died, *"He told us one more time how to get there, and went home and went!"*

What a quaint but beautiful way to say it! And what's more beautiful is that *Mom and Dad were brought together again the night he went to be with the Lord!* Now they are together with the Lord, Whom they served together for nearly a half a century.

Before our Lord Jesus returned to the Father after His sojourn on earth, He said to His disciples, *"Where I go, you know, and the way you know."* Then He added, *"I am the Way, the Truth, and the Life..."*

Where our mother and father went, when their life here on earth had ended, we children know, and the Way we know!

And in response to their teaching and guiding us, we are confident that we will join them in the "Heavenly Father's House," the one Place where the hospitality is greater than it was in the parsonage where I grew up with our dear mother and father.

CHAPTER THIRTY-SEVEN

RUNAWAY HORSES

As I am writing this in Arizona in the winter of 2007, a serious accident occurred a few days ago in a parade in nearby Tucson involving runaway horses.

In the annual rodeo parade in Tucson, called *La Fiesta de los Vaquaros* (The Festival of the Cowboys), only horses are used; there are no motor-driven vehicles at all. I think it's the only parade of its kind in the United States. It's a very beautiful and interesting parade.

About one thousand horses are ridden or used in harness in this rodeo parade in Tucson. Many of them are beautiful show horses, some are from the last U.S. Army Cavalry Unit (at Fort Huachuca, Arizona), and some are workhorses. The workhorses too are majestic looking animals, but they are more easily *spooked* because they are not accustomed to being around crowds of people.

What occurred a few days ago in the Tucson parade was indeed tragic; it caused the death of a little girl. The runaway horses knocked the girl off the horse she was riding next to her parents and trampled her. It all happened so fast; it was over before anyone could react.

Those powerful animals can go berserk so quickly and cause problems. I found that out while working on a threshing crew north of Odessa, about ten miles east of Ortonville.

I believe it was in 1947. I was a college student at Concordia in St. Paul at the time, studying for the ministry. I was just home for the summer, trying to earn enough to pay my room and board for another year of college.

The runaway incident with horses, which I experienced, took place while I was working for a farmer by the name of Bernie Swenson, whose wife, Carol, was from the Holman family, neighbors of ours in Odessa.

Although I often rode workhorses (always bareback), I actually had a fear of horses, and it seems they knew it.

For example, one day, while I was putting harnesses on a team in a stall in the barn, they squeezed me between them till I was almost lifted off the ground and out of breath! I thought I saw *a smile on the horses' faces* after they did that. Maybe they were saying, in their way, "So there, kid; smarter we may not be, but bigger and more powerful we are!"

The runaway I experienced occurred when we were threshing flax. Flax bundles were incredibly *"sticky,"* the flax heads getting tangled up with each other like they didn't want to be taken to the threshing machine.

Because the bundles clung like that to each other, we tried never to stand on a load of flax in the hayrack. The seat above the front of the rack (I called it *a perch*) was rarely used, but it came in handy when we were threshing flax, so we wouldn't have to stand on the load and trample down the bundles.

If we'd stand on a load of flax, like we did on wheat, oats, or barley, it could *make a preacher cuss on Sunday* when we were trying to get the bundles apart at the threshing machine. Riding on that perch minimized the problem.

While sitting up there on that seat one afternoon, I was driving the team with a load of flax across a field toward the farm buildings where the threshing machine was set up. Unfortunately, I took a little shortcut instead of staying on *the tracks* made by other wagons.

All of a sudden, one of the steel wheels on the front of the wagon hit a rock protruding out of the ground. There was a loud *clang!* At the same time, the tongue of the wagon (a long pole between the team of horses) nudged the side of one of the horses!

The horses jumped! The wagon lurched, and I fell backward into the load! With the reins loose, the horses started to run and soon were in a dead gallop even though they were in harness, pulling a wagonload of bundles!

Before I could even get to my knees, in the middle of the load, now *flying across the field*, the horses ran *as though crazy* through an open gate! Then, for some reason, they turned sharply, dumping the hayrack upside down off the wheels and frame, with me under the load!

I saw nothing after that! I was trapped under the load! One of the men who was more or less following me with his load saw what happened and told me.

After dumping the load, and me with it, the horses, pulling only the wheels and frame of the wagon, ran toward the threshing machine! Fortunately, there was a load of bundles in their way. They galloped, smack into that load, almost like they were so blinded by their excitement that they didn't see it! Both horses fell and got tangled up in their harnesses!

It was good that the load they hit was there! If the horses, running crazy like that, had run into the long belt between the large tractor power source and the threshing machine, they could both have been killed or seriously injured!

One of the men, a seasoned horse handler, came running and was able to get the team calmed down as they were getting back to their feet! By this time, the men around the threshing machine stopped everything and ran looking for me! Seeing the wagon without the rack, they didn't know what had happened!

On the other side of the barn, they found the rack of flax bundles upside down and heard me making muffled sounds from underneath it all! Hurriedly, the men got the rack tipped upright and dug me out of the load!

There I was, fortunately with only a few bruises. What I had hurt the most was my pride! I should have been more firmly seated on *the perch* with the reins in hand, and I shouldn't have taken the shortcut across the field where the steel wheel of the wagon hit the rock.

After the men found that I was not seriously injured, I got more kidding from them than I had gotten in a long time.

One of the farmhands who knew that I didn't care much to work with horses said to me, "Ya see, *Mr. College Egghead,* them's not dumb animals. They never went to school, but they got some smarts—horse sense, ya might say. They know who likes 'em and who don't! They was jus' getting' even with ya today!"

Maybe he was right.

Horses are beautiful and very powerful animals, but they certainly have their own way of dealing with emergencies.

CHAPTER THIRTY-EIGHT

MOVIES IN OUR LIFE WHEN WE WERE KIDS

We didn't see many movies when we were kids in Odessa in the thirties and forties. In fact, I remember that when I went to prep school in St. Paul in 1944 when I was fifteen years old, I was asked by a roommate if I had seen a certain movie. I said I had not. Then he asked me about another one. When I said no again, the boy asked me how many movies I had ever seen. I was able to count them, so it wasn't many.

We didn't miss not seeing movies. It's like I remember Mom saying many years later, when asked whether she missed not having an automatic washer: "What you've never had, you don't miss." How true!

In chapter 19 of this book, about *summer evenings in Odessa* when we were children, I said that there were plenty of things to do before television and all the other things children and young people have today. It's so true that *what you've never had, you don't miss.*

We had radio, but that was not an attraction like movies and televisions are today. We did listen to some programs, usually as a family. There was Fred Waring, Kate Smith, and the Longine Symphonet for music, and Henry Aldrich, George Burns, and Jack Benny for laughs. There were others, of course, but not many that attracted us.

Mom also listened to two fifteen-minute soap operas in the daytime. That was her rest time around noon. I think she slept on the couch through both of them. Dad listened to the news broadcasts, and to be sure, he did not sleep through them. He was very much interested in what was going on in the world. No one in our family, however, bent his or her ears toward the radio like people focus their eyes on television for hours at a time today.

I'll admit that television is a wonderful learning tool today, but is that what most people use it for? Do they watch programs that would expand their horizon, or do they watch primarily to be entertained? I wonder.

Children can learn so much from the *Sesame Street* program, *Mister Rogers' Neighborhood*, and others. Teenagers and adults can also learn much from the History Channel and educational programs on public television.

It's amazing how we can see animals, birds, and insects in their natural habitat right before our eyes! Not long ago, my wife and I saw a program about penguins. It was wonderful to see those interesting creatures so close-up. How many people would be able to visit Antarctica to do that? Yet there we were—watching as though we were right there with those amazing creatures!

Also, stories like *Little House on the Prairie* and *The Waltons* and *Bonanza* can show us much about life years—even a century—ago.

There are programs, too, that bring other parts of the world into our living rooms, especially the news programs today. It's like we're taking an airplane ride to various parts of the world.

There was a movie theater in Ortonville, and we did see a few movies there. I think the first one was Walt Disney's *Snow White and the Seven Dwarfs*. Also, I remember seeing a Shirley Temple movie. I don't remember the name of it, but I do recall that we were surprised that such a young girl could act, like she did. (I believe Shirley Temple was born the same year I was—1928.)

One thing also that impressed me in the movie theaters were the newsreels shown before the movie started. It was as though we were in another city or country, watching what was happening. We see that sort of thing every time we turn on the TV now, but that was so unusual for us to see on the screen in a theater.

The funniest movies we saw were those with Abbot and Costello. *Those men were funny!* They had the Ortonville movie house *rocking with laughter*. There were a few other comedies that we saw, but Abbot and Costello topped them all, in my opinion. We enjoyed them even more than Bob Hope. Maybe the nature of the comedy in Abbot and Costello movies appealed more to kids.

In the 1960s, when my brother Danny was at the height of his career as a songwriter in California, a son of Bud Abbot, who was a friend of Danny's, came to my brother's house in Tarzana, California, to show one of the old Abbot and Costello movies, and he gave each of us who were there that evening a '78 record of the *Who's on First?* routine, Abbot and Costello's most famous.

I told that son of Bud Abbott that evening how the people in the Ortonville theater almost *died of laughter* when those movies were shown. He seemed quite pleased to know that and said that he would tell his father, who was very sick at that time. (His father, Bud Abbot, died not too long after that.)

I think the most regular moviegoers in Odessa were Mr. and Mrs. Shellenbarger. They went to the theater in Ortonville almost every Sunday evening. They were nice enough to take Manny and me along a few times. I remember that Manny and I, in Shellenbarger's backseat, were talking all the way back to Odessa about the movie we had seen.

The Shellenbargers never said much, as I recall, but I'm sure they enjoyed the movie too because they kept on going back almost every Sunday night. Of course, there's a possibility that they enjoyed hearing a "rerun" of the movie from Manny and me, as we retold it to each other in their backseat.

In the late thirties and early forties, we saw some good war movies. One in particular had Greer Garson in it. I think it was called *Mrs. Miniver*. We were really moved by that one, and it brought the war *a little closer to home.*

Also, the newsreels during the war helped us to understand more of what was happening in various parts of the world. We had heard things from soldiers who had come home on furlough, but it was not as vivid to hear about it as it was to see things shown on the screen.

There were a few free movies shown outside in the Odessa square when we were kids. We enjoyed them, but they were never the latest movies, and it was somewhat frustrating that things went wrong with the projectors so often. Also, it wasn't the greatest to have to sit on the grass and swat mosquitoes while seeing the movie.

It's interesting how the technology has changed so much since we were kids in the thirties and forties. That certainly is true in the entertainment business. However, like in so many other things, along with the advantages, have come some disadvantages.

Our children today have so many blessings in what they can see on television and in the movies. Of course, we know that not all they see is good for them.

Also, so much of what they can see and hear today perhaps keeps them too inactive physically. I hope the children today in the Odessa area still get outside occasionally to skate on the river, go sliding on the hills, or play basketball outside in the cold till the ball loses its bounce and has to be warmed up inside.

They may not see too much of what's happening in the world on the river, the hills, or on the backyard basketball courts; but more outside activity would be good for them in many ways.

We did enjoy the movies when we were kids, but there was not the temptation to spend too much of our time with our eyes fixed on the theater or television screens. The outside beckoned to us, and I believe that was good.

CHAPTER THIRTY-NINE

TEACHING IN A ONE-ROOM SCHOOL WHILE STILL GROWING UP (IN MORE WAYS THAN ONE)

Perhaps this chapter does not belong in this book about my *growing-up years*. I was nineteen, just short of twenty, when I began teaching in a one-room school. Also, the teaching was not done in western Minnesota where I spent the first years of my life, but in northeast Wisconsin, about thirty miles from Green Bay.

My oldest brother, Ihno, however, would vote, I'm sure, for my including this experience as a part of my *growing up*. He told me that it was his opinion that *I grew up ten years in the two calendar years that I taught* in that one-room school, from 1948 to '50.

I'm not certain that he was right about that, but I do know that in those two years, the Lord gave me direction for the rest of my life. The teaching experience was very interesting and helpful for later years. Also, I was drawn very close to God through dealing with those children and was convinced that the Lord did want me to work in the ministry.

After those two years of teaching, it was my hope and prayer that one day, teaching and the pastoral ministry would somehow be combined in my life. It certainly was, when I taught at a college in Southern Arizona and still worked in the ministry in various ways, including conducting a prison ministry and a Christian youth camp for a number of years.

So how did this phase of my life—teaching in a one-room school—come about? In the fall of 1947, when I was beginning the last year of studies at Concordia, St.Paul (the *sophomore year of college,* at that time), members of our class were asked to volunteer to take a year out to teach in the Lutheran school system before entering the seminary at St. Louis.

The offer was that extra classes in education would be given to the volunteers during the school year by professors of education, including several from of the University of Minnesota. Also, an eight-week summer session in education would be given in 1948, with expenses paid. In addition to this, one year of teaching would be counted as the year of vicarage (something like an internship), which is always required before graduation from the seminary.

I volunteered to join those who were accepting this offer for several reasons. The primary reason was that I thought perhaps my calling would not only be to the *pastoral ministry* but also to the *teaching ministry*. It was also my feeling that during a year of teaching, the Lord would show me what His will was for my life.

My prayers were definitely answered during that time. I was assigned to a one-room school between Shawano and Clintonville, Wisconsin, where I taught six grades in a one-room school for two years, from 1948 to 1950.

During the first year of teaching I was also enrolled for vicarage at Concordia Seminary, St. Louis, and I sent in reports as a vicar. The second year I stayed at that little Christian day school because it would otherwise have closed. The reason was that the request of the sponsoring congregation, St. Martin's Lutheran Church, for a student teacher was not filled.

In addition to the other advantages of teaching those two years, friendships were formed with people in that Christian community which continued throughout the decades following, and some have continued even to this day, more than a half century later. I thank God that I was led to volunteer for that extra education and the teaching experience when I was just a sophomore in college.

Incidentally, I actually was still *growing up physically* at that time. I increased in height *over an inch* during that first year of teaching. Some of the people in the St. Martin's congregation thought I looked more like an *elementary student* myself than *a teacher* when I arrived there in August of 1948.

Maybe they were right. However, I did succeed. I may not have been the greatest teacher those kids ever had, but the children and I got along well enough. In fact, *I never used any corporal punishment* although I was given a willow switch before I started and was told to use it.

There were a few other reasons why I had some success in spite of my youth. One was that I asked for help in how to teach *six grades in one room*, and I got it from a woman who had taught in one-room schools for fifty years.

In one week she taught me how to group children together from various grades and how to teach the children to tutor fellow pupils in various ways. There was a *constant hubbub* in that schoolroom because so much was going on, but the children handled the situations fairly well.

I dealt with the children with reason and God's Word, very much as my parents dealt with us in our large family. Also, I remembered the teachers I had had (when I was in school) who I thought were good—and why I thought so.

Another thing which helped me have a good relationship with the children was that I taught the children how to play various games, including softball, and played with them. Also, they appreciated very much that I taught them to sing. They *learned harmony* reasonably well through my starting them with *rounds*. (I rewrote every round I knew, giving them Christian words.)

By Christmas of the first year, I had them singing in two-part harmony, and I sang with them, adding the third part. I was not a musician. I did most of the teaching of music with my voice and a pitch pipe. It worked reasonably well, I guess.

Also, believe it or not, sometimes when the snow was right for snowballs, we built a fort; I was on one side, all the children on the other. I let them all throw snowballs at me while I tried (but not too hard) to duck and dodge. They loved it, especially when they succeeded in hitting me! When we went inside after playing together like that, everything was *business* again; that they knew!

The children obviously learned something. A number of them earned college degrees and became professionals in various fields. I still hear from several of those former students every Christmas.

Now that I have written this chapter, I have decided that it *does* belong in this book about my growing up, even though it involved the years in my life from nineteen to twenty-one.

Anyone who would like to read more about the two years I taught in this one-room school can look for a *fiction novel* I have written based on those two years called *Grass Lake Junction*. Also, some of the more humorous occurrences are included in a book I have written called *HUMOR FROM THE CLASSROOM and Other Places I've Hung Out Over the Years*. For that book, I drew humor from *all my nearly forty years of teaching*; some, however, is from my years in the one-room school mentioned here.

CHAPTER FORTY

BEGINNING TO PREPARE FOR THE MINISTRY AS A YOUNG BOY

When I was a child, I knew that I wanted to be a pastor, like my father was. In fact, it was somehow instilled in me that *the Lord wanted me* to be in the ministry.

Our father was sure that all his five sons were brought into this world to be pastors. He felt that they were chosen, like Jeremiah was *"from the mother's womb."* Our mother seemed to have a similar thought; her father also was a pastor, as was her oldest brother. She, like our dad, felt that the ministry was *the highest calling.*

Interestingly, our father did not come to America from Germany *to study for the ministry.* When he immigrated in 1907, at age nineteen, it was his hope to study to become an architect. He had been a ship's carpenter in the shipbuilding port of Wihelmshaven on the North Sea in Germany.

He had done well in the special carpentry involved in building German ships and was hoping he could become a designer of the carpentry in ships. This was the dream he had told his aunt and uncle about when they said they would sponsor his coming to America.

It seems that they didn't think too much of his *dream,* however, but didn't tell him. When he arrived in Wisconsin, from Germany, it became apparent that his aunt and uncle *wanted him to be a farmer.* Although *his aunt and uncle never said* so, it seems that they wanted him to be *the son they never had.*

His first two years in America was a time of bitter disappointment. The aunt and uncle kept him almost like a servant and treated him as such. He said he would perhaps have gone back to Germany, but he had no money, often not a cent to his name.

That was when he had a religious experience. While walking, probably with his head down in despair, back from Merrill one Sunday to his relatives' farm in Pine River, he came upon an outdoor Lutheran mission festival service in a clearing in the woods. A missionary from South America was preaching *in German* about his bringing the message of forgiveness of God in Christ to people in Brazil.

Dad said that hearing the missionary's message brought back memories of his attending worship as a child. As he listened to the missionary preach while he stood *alone away from the people,* he gave his heart to Christ and told the Lord that he wanted to serve Him.

It was also a result of that religious experience and his subsequently going to church in Pine River that he met Minnie Thormaehlen, the daughter of a pastor who became his wife about seven years later. His relationship with Minnie started when her father asked his daughter to help young Ihno learn English. At that time, Minnie was fourteen, and Ihno was twenty.

In 1916, when she was twenty-three and he was twenty-nine, they were married—in Yellow Bank Township, Minnesota, near the South Dakota border, where Minnie's father had come to serve Immanuel Lutheran Church. Dad had graduated from the seminary in 1915.

The first child, Ruth, was born in 1917; the first son, Ihno Junior, was born in 1918. Ruth and Ihno graduated from high school in Odessa in 1935, seven years after Dad came to serve Trinity Lutheran Church in Odessa.

Ruth, the oldest child in our family, was the first to leave our parsonage home. She attended the Normal School in Ortonville and taught in a one-room school north of Odessa. Later, after receiving more education, she taught in Lutheran schools. She learned piano from our mother and became quite an accomplished church organist years later.

Our brother Ihno, the oldest son in our family, worked at Kollitz's Store in Odessa for two years after high school. In 1937, he left home to begin studying for the ministry.

Ihno had been like a *young father* to the youngest of us in the family. We idolized him, so we hated to see him leave home. However, we knew he would be a wonderful pastor.

That fall, after Ihno left home, though I was only nine, I started to accompany Dad on his pastoral calls whenever I could. Even when he was called out in the middle of the night, I got up and got ready to go with him.

"But you have to go to school in the morning," Mom would tell me. My answer was usually, "Somebody has to be with Dad, in case anything happens in the night." Really, I wanted to tell her I was starting to prepare for the ministry, but I thought she would laugh since I was so young.

One such night, I accompanied our father when he was called to minister to Grandma Hahmann on her deathbed. A young man, who I think was one of Grandma Hahmann's sons, noticed how I stayed next to Dad and observed him closely. He saw too how I listened to Dad's every word as he ministered to the dying woman and the family.

As Dad and I were leaving, the man asked me *in German* if I was going to be a pastor like my father. I looked up at him and said, "Das hof' ich." (I hope so.) I'll never forget how he smiled when he heard me say that, though I spoke ever so shyly, hoping he wasn't going to laugh.

To my surprise, he patted me on the head and told me that if I would be half the *Sehlsorger* (carer of souls) my father was, I would be a good pastor. That made me feel good, as Dad took me by the hand and went out to start up our Chevy to head home in the wee hours of the morning.

I was very pleased that the man felt that way about my father; that was what I thought too. In fact, when Dad raised his arms to pronounce the benediction in a worship service, I thought he could have *parted the Red Sea* like Moses did when he led the children of Israel out of Egypt.

I can still see him with his arms raised over the congregation and hear him chant the benediction in German: "Der Herr segne dich und behuete dich " . . ." (The Lord bless you and keep you . . .) "There," I always thought, "is a real *man of God!*" I knew Dad wasn't perfect, but I felt he was *specially chosen* to serve the Lord.

When I did janitorial work in the church—building fires in the church stove or cleaning—I would sometimes step into the pulpit, *if I was alone,* and say a few words I had heard Dad say the previous Sunday. I made sure no one saw me, though. I didn't want them to think I was being silly since I was just a boy.

When I was alone in the church, I'd also sometimes sit in a pew for a few minutes or kneel at the altar. I knew that the Lord was *always with me*, but when I was the only one in the church, I felt as though I was the only person in the world He was paying attention to at that moment.

At times, also when I was walking my paper route in the twilight of a winter evening, I'd stand on a snowbank while bringing the papers to Richard Menzel and Frank

Gutzman on the outskirts of Odessa. There I would preach a few sentences I'd heard the Sunday before.

It seemed that a few rabbits in the snow or chickadees on a tree limb were listening. At least I hoped so, and I wondered if one day I would actually preach my own sermon of the Gospel of Christ *to people in a church*.

In the confirmation classes when I was twelve and thirteen, I sometimes wondered while listening to Dad whether one day I'd be teaching God's Word to *a child of mine*. It seemed a little ridiculous when I was so young, so I never told anyone.

My studies for the ministry finally began formally in the fall of 1944, just before I turned sixteen. I enrolled at Concordia Academy in St. Paul as a junior in high school.

Then followed college, two years of teaching in a one-room school, another year of teaching in the city of Philadelphia, Pennsylvania, followed by years of theological studies at a seminary, and graduate school at a university.

I was finally ordained in 1956. The night before the day of my ordination, my father walked with me for several hours through the northern Indiana village of Westville (in some respects, a town like Odessa) where I was to be ordained the next day. As we walked, Dad shared with me many of his thoughts regarding the Christian ministry.

The wisdom he shared with me that summer evening was, I'm sure, as valuable as years of seminary and theological discussions led by learned professors.

Among the things he said, I'll never forget how he said something like this: "No matter what your sermon text is, remember to tell the person who may have entered the church for the first—and perhaps the last—time, *the way to eternal life in Jesus the Savior.*

The next day my father preached the ordination sermon based on the Old Testament:

"But the Lord said unto me, Say not, I am a child, for thou shalt go to all that I shall send thee, and whatsoever I command thee, thou shalt speak. Be not afraid of their faces, for I am with thee to deliver thee, saith the Lord. Then the Lord put forth His hand and touched my mouth. And the Lord said, Behold I have put My words in thy mouth" (Jeremiah 1:7-9).

After he preached the sermon, my father, seven other pastors, and church officials put their hands on my head in the ceremony for the ordination blessing. I felt that I was finally taken by the Lord's hand into the ministry in His Kingdom.

Though I knew that I was a sinner, I felt the Savior wanted to use me to preach and teach the Gospel to all who would hear, young and old, *and I knew, too, that I had to preach to myself,* for I, too, needed to be reminded of my salvation in Christ.

It was made complete when the congregation, in that ordination service, which included my mother, several brothers and sisters, other loved ones, and friends sang "God of the Prophets, Bless the Prophets' Sons."

CHAPTER FORTY-ONE

WANDERING THE STREETS OF ODESSA AT AGE SEVENTY-FIVE

In May of 2003, brother Ihno, sister Marcia, and I visited Odessa for a few days. On Sunday morning, we had a very meaningful service at Trinity in which Ihno preached, and I conducted the communion service. Old friends of our family came from various places in Minnesota and eastern South Dakota to be with us that day. It was truly a day to remember!

The next afternoon, when Ihno was resting, and Marty was visiting with friends, I took the opportunity to wander slowly around Odessa, our old hometown, by myself.

In 1988, fifteen years earlier, members of Trinity Lutheran Church asked me to retire in Odessa and to serve part-time as pastor of Trinity Church, the church of which our father was pastor from 1927 to 1947.

I was not quite ready at that time to retire from my teaching position at Cochise College in Douglas, Arizona.

I told them that, and I gave them several other reasons for my reluctance to go to live in Odessa.

The Odessa people knew that I had in mind to write, in my retirement, about my growing up in the parsonage of Trinity Church. Consequently, members of the church suggested that *it would be the best for me to be in Odessa in order to write about my growing up there.* In answer to that, I told them that *the village of Odessa in which I grew up,* in the 1930s and early '40s, *is more fixed in my mind today, than it exists in reality.*

I'm sure that it would have been interesting to serve the Trinity congregation, though it is totally different in many respects from what it was when my father was the pastor there. However, I did not feel that being in Odessa would help me much in my writing since everything is so different today in the village.

In my nostalgic trip around the town that May day in 2003, I was more convinced along the way that I was right. Odessa is a different place today, and it isn't different merely because I am a different person after all these years. It has so thoroughly changed.

In 1930, just two years after I was born in Odessa, the population was listed in the U.S. Census as 316. Today, the sign on the edge of town lists the population as 113.

Although that's a difference of only slightly over two hundred people, it's more than half of what the population was! Furthermore, the whole nature of the village has changed from what it was over six decades ago.

The farmers and the village residents did most of their trading in Odessa when I was a child, and I'm told that *there were nearly ten times as many farm families in the '30s and '40s as there are today.* The farms are much larger, and they need fewer people to work them.

Transportation also is so different today. More primitive vehicles and poor roads made transportation slower and more difficult decades ago.

For example, Ortonville, a thriving city of two thousand in the 1930s, was forty-five minutes away from Odessa sixty years ago—more in bad weather, or when the roads were muddy or covered with snow or ice. Today the towns are *ten minutes apart* with modern vehicles, in all but the most inclement weather conditions.

Back to my slow, nostalgic trip around the village. At the corner by the church, I let my imagination roam. Trinity Church and the old parsonage do not look today like they did decades ago. Both have been extensively remodeled.

I know the church building is much more utilitarian today, with its basement parish hall and roomy narthex. However, I miss the high steeple and the old high windows on the church. It doesn't look much like the church in which we worshiped those many years ago.

I don't mean to say that the church would be better as it was many years ago; I'm just saying that what I see there today does not conjure up memories of my childhood like the old building would.

Also, the little church school and the outbuildings are gone. I guess that, too, is an improvement, but it seems strange to see the yard the way it is today. The square where we played kitten ball and the shed where our basketball backboard was, are gone. The memories of our good times there are still vivid, because in my mind, it's all still there.

Also, the little school where so many catechism and summer Bible school classes were taught has vanished in reality, but not from my memories.

As I was leaving the corner by the church, I thought I heard my father chant the benediction in German and the parishioners sing their response. In fact, it seemed like I could, off in the distance, hear the children sing a Christmas carol even though it was the middle of the May.

As I passed the parsonage, I imagined our large family having Sunday dinner together, with Dad asking us what he preached about. How strange it is to see the parsonage stand empty today!

The hill past where Dreffeenes and Von Eschons lived was all grass, and the barbed-wire fence was tightly closed to keep the cattle securely inside. How alive that hill was with children on sleds many years ago when there was snow in the winter!

I went along the road, going by Aarndts' house, where it seemed Clara was gathering eggs in their henhouse, getting ready to bring a couple dozen eggs to the parsonage for the large family that meant so much to her.

Then I drove up to the cemetery, God's Acre, on the hill, where so many of the faithful from Trinity Church were laid to rest, at the end of their labors here on earth.

I thought about how, when I worked as the janitor for Trinity Church, I rang the bells for some of those funerals, beginning with the service for Grandpa Aarndt, the best ringer of the bells many years ago even when he was quite elderly.

At the cemetery, I walked past the graves of so many I had known. Then I visited the tiny grave of our little brother Waldemar, who was taken by the Lord to be with Him in heaven such a short time after he was born.

I wondered what it would have been like to have had Waldemar grow up with us. As Janssen sibling number 8, he would have been between Manny and Danny in age. It certainly would have been different with *four little boys* at the bottom of the family instead of only three. Maybe there would have been *two pairs* of boys, rather than *four little boys*. I wondered what that would have been like.

As I stood there in the cemetery, imagining, I thought of the words of the poet Whittier in "Maud Muller" where he wrote, *"Of all sad words of tongue and pen, the saddest are these: it might have been."* Then I wondered: "Who are we, anyway, to question the Lord's will?" *He certainly knows better than we do, what is best!*

I bowed my head in prayer at Waldemar's grave, thanking the Lord for His grace and mercy and asking Him to gather us all in eternity for *the greatest family reunion we could ever have.*

After my prayer, I lifted my head and looked across the field from the cemetery where you could, years ago, see the Odessa school. It seemed so different that it was no longer there. I tearfully uttered, "It's gone from the face of the earth! No more happy voices in the schoolyard and no more sliding happily down the hill after school!"

As I descended the hill again from the cemetery, I went past where the Tesch family lived years ago. I remembered how Earl and Elmer Tesch could draw horses with a pencil—horses that looked so real that it seemed the animals could run off the piece of paper on which they were drawn.

Yet I recalled one teacher who rarely, if ever, praised them for their artistic ability. Most of the time, she told the Tesch boys, rather, that they should quit wasting their time drawing and do their arithmetic homework!

That reminded me of reading about when Walt Disney was a boy. Disney was told angrily by his own father that his drawing pictures was a waste of time! Yet it's a more enjoyable world because Walt Disney kept on drawing.

I don't know what happened to the Tesch boys. Did they ever do anything in art? I wonder.

As I went slowly past the next corner, I almost thought I saw Donny Anderson on the porch, putting together one of his many model airplanes. His friends laughed when they heard Donny say that he was going to be a pilot one day.

No one realized that Donny would have his opportunity in World War II. Horrible as the war was, it changed so many things for so many people in a number of ways! Consider how farmer boy Harvey Pansch went from little Odessa to being an ace pilot for the U.S. Air Force in that war.

As I came close to the railroad tracks on the edge of the village, I remembered how Frank Gutzman, a section foreman for the Milwaukee Road, was always so concerned about the safety of the trains as he watched them go by his house every evening and heard them pass in the night.

I recalled, too, how Mr. Gutzman always said when he lost a hand in *the game of Rook* that *what he lost in peanuts, he would make up in bananas.* That always made our dad smile, especially if he was Frank's partner, losing with him.

As I came toward downtown Odessa, I passed where Leander Strei's filling station originally was, on the east side of downtown.

I smiled as I recalled that in that little station, along with products for cars, Leander sold gallon jugs of Master Liquid Hog Medicine, advertised by George B. German who sang Western songs early on summer mornings on WNAX, Yankton, South Dakota.

It's strange what comes from the northwest corner of your head when you're reminiscing all by yourself.

When I mentioned to my older brother Ihno what came to my mind about Leander's station, he told me that Leander Strei was quite a basketball player at Odessa High School in his day.

In fact, in a high school game in 1932, Leander *set a record for Odessa*. It was a game against Ortonville, a larger school. Remember that the gymnasiums were smaller at that time, and the rules of the game of basketball were quite different. Consequently, scores were lower.

That game with Ortonville, played in the old town hall in Odessa, in January of 1932 *was tied at nine in regulation.* Odessa won in overtime, twelve to eleven, and amazingly, *Leander scored all twelve points for Odessa! Maybe that's a record that still stands—scoring all the points in a game!*

Back to my slow journey around Odessa in 2003: Not far from Leander's station, across the tracks from the old stockyard, was Hugo Menzel's place. He had a few cows many years ago, and we got our milk from him for a number of years. I think it was his contribution to the pastor's family.

I recalled how brother Vernon and I were getting the milk in tin gallon pails from there one morning before school. A freight train was slowly moving back and forth, switching freight cars on the sidetracks. They blocked our way, and the train was too long for us to go around—at least to make it home and then to school on time.

Vernon suggested that we climb up the ladder on a freight car and go over the top. That's what we did, but when we got on the top of the freight car, there was a clang on the hitch, and we were moving!

We fortunately didn't fall. We quickly got down the other side of the car, and were both able to jump off before the train got to moving too fast.

A few days later, there was a message received at the Odessa school warning *the boys who were "playing around the freight trains early in the morning."* Lucky for Vernon and me—the school authorities never did find out who those boys were, nor did Dad and Mom.

Next, in my slow journey around Odessa, I came downtown, where there just isn't much anymore.

I recalled how August Anderson, many years ago, had his blacksmith shop across from Luenbergs' harness shop. Augie, a lame man who *walked more upright than many men*, always sang as he worked. You could usually hear his strong, happy voice over the clanging and banging of his work, repairing plowshares for farmers.

Mr. Anderson's blacksmith shop was later moved to the old firehouse, next to the old town hall. Our brother Ihno said that, prior to 1936, at the time that the high school team still played their games in the old town hall, they dressed for their games in that firehouse (even when it was below zero), hanging their clothes on the ladders on the side of the truck.

Ihno said they always hoped there wouldn't be a fire during the game, or their clothes may end up at the scene of the fire, or fly off on the way.

That reminds me of how we always said that when the volunteer fire department in Odessa got a call, the first thing they did was pump up the tires up on the truck. (It wasn't that bad; that was just a local joke.)

That reminds me of a comedian years ago who said he had the highest regard for the *volunteer fire department* in his hometown in Indiana. What he said went something like this: *"Aunt Tillie's house would've burned down in ten minutes, but the volunteer fire department kept it going all night."*

It's sad that there isn't much downtown anymore. Almost the entire main street is gone—Kollitzes, the pool hall, Batson's store, Happy Steffen's garage, and other buildings. I'm glad there still is a little restaurant downtown in Odessa. It's almost all there is, and it still serves as a gathering place.

As I passed the building where Kollitz's store was, I thought of how I stopped at Kollitz's in 1964, twenty years after I left home to enroll at Concordia in St. Paul and seventeen years after our family moved out of Odessa.

I took a briefcase with me into the store and asked for Leonard Kollitz. When he appeared, I said, "You are Leonard Kollitz?" Nervously, he said, "Yes." Then I said, as seriously as I could, "I'm from the FBI."

He invited me to his office, away from the few others in the store. Somehow, seeing how apprehensive he was, I couldn't continue what I had planned. So I said, "You don't know who I am, do you?"

Still nervous, he said, "No, I don't." Starting to laugh, I said, "I'm Arlo Janssen." Then, feeling relieved, I guess, he laughed a little too.

After chatting for a few minutes, I said, "Do you remember that you wouldn't hire me when I was a teenager because you said I never took anything seriously?"

It didn't take him long to come back with, *"Apparently you still don't!"* What could I say? It was good to see him, though, and chat a few minutes about old times. The one in our family Leonard asked about the most was Ihno, our oldest brother who worked at the store for several years before he went to college in 1937.

One building still standing downtown is the post office, but it surely must have fewer people who get their mail there than when our family had Box 31.

In fact, there isn't much left at all in Odessa. Small as it was, *it was alive in the '30s and '40s, especially on Wednesday and Saturday nights.* How well I remember that! An awful lot of people came to town those nights.

I also went down the street, past where the old town hall once stood, and drove around the old town square, a little south of downtown. I recalled how that square was used for high school activities—track meets, baseball games, and tennis matches. Also, there were town team baseball games held there many Sunday afternoons in the summer.

As I stopped there for a few minutes, I thought I heard Walter Bumstead sing "When It's Springtime in the Rockies" on the pitcher's mound between innings so they would give him a cracked bat he had asked for. *How long ago was that?*

Finally, I headed out of the village again, passing the new town hall, built by the hardworking WPA men in 1936. (Was it really that long ago?) How the time passes! Going slowly out of town, I imagined that I heard Mr. Semmler tapping nails into shoes he was repairing in the shop in his home, on the edge of town.

On my way back to Ortonville, where we were staying, I wondered if there are children in Odessa today who get away from TV and video games, at least occasionally, to go sliding on the hill or skating at the river. I also wondered if there is sometimes today an echo of laughter of farm families meeting in the streets on Wednesday and Saturday nights.

If I had retired in Odessa, I suppose I could have *imagined* a lot of things for my writing like I did that May day in 2003. Oh well, it's too late now; I'm much older, and anyway, they now have a pastor for Trinity Church.

The next day, Ihno, Marty, and I spent a good part of the day visiting and having prayer with old friends and acquaintances who were residing in the twilight of their years at Northridge Care Center in Ortonville. It was a day of ambivalence—spiritually joyful, yet rather sad to see those folks in a rest home.

The day after that, we returned to Hastings, Minnesota, where sister Marty lives. The next day, Ihno and I returned to California and Arizona with a mixture of sadness and thanksgiving to God for His goodness and grace for all of us.

While flying back to Arizona, I looked out of the window, at about thirty thousand feet, recalling how a pilot landed a small canvas-sided plane on the school hill in Odessa in about 1935 and gave rides for two dollars, which not many people could afford.

I remembered how an old man thumped the drumlike side of that plane while the pilot was helping another passenger aboard and said, "Humbug!" I don't think that old man saw many more changes in technology before *the church bells tolled for him.*

Now, back in Arizona, a land I've called home for nearly fifty years, each time I go back in memory to Odessa, *the world* in which we grew up, I thank God for all that the town and its people meant to us when we lived there. Also, I thank God that we still have friends in that little town and the surrounding area.

"One day, we'll all be with the Lord," our pastor father often said, "and then we'll wonder why we wanted to stay here on earth so long."

When we are with the Lord, I know we'll see the old friends from Odessa, those who worshiped with us and some for whom I tolled the bells when I was the janitor of the church.

EPILOGUE

IT WAS ALL WORTHWHILE, AND I THANK GOD FOR IT.

As I have said, the little town of Odessa was *our world* during our growing-up years. We knew the town well, every nook and cranny of it.

In fact, for a class in about the sixth grade in the school in Odessa, I attempted to draw a map of the entire town, including every building—the outhouses, barns, and woodsheds, as well as houses and businesses.

I don't know how accurate my drawing was, but I do know that I knew where every building was. If I didn't know that before, I certainly became acquainted with everything in the town when I was the town's only paperboy, making shortcuts through yards and down alleys every day for several years.

Odessa was not just a group of buildings, however. It was a community of people who lived in the town and in the surrounding area. We, of course, were aware of there being a big wide world, but to us, while we were growing up, it seemed Odessa was in the center of it.

My writing about my early years has made me very much aware of the importance of all the people we knew and the assurance that God looked after all of us in that little town.

I have never regretted being born and growing up in Odessa. And I certainly have never regretted being brought up in a parsonage with a large family and parents who always strived to live close to God, in appreciation for the salvation they knew in Jesus Christ, the Savior.

When I am asked, "Did you like growing up in a parsonage?" I jokingly answer, "What choice did I have?"

Also, I have been asked many times if I liked being a part of a large family. Also, to that, I answer, "Being number 7, what choice did I have?"

Seriously, I wouldn't have traded either of those things for anything. I felt blessed to be brought up in a parsonage by Christian parents, and I always felt blessed to be a part of a large family.

We often joked that life in our big family was a "share and share alike" existence; *you share it, and I'll like it*. In reality, *it was truly a share and share alike life*. That played itself out during our entire lifetime, from dividing cookies or sharing toys when we were small to helping each other during our education years and all along the way when there was a need.

If it takes a village to rear a child, it takes a Christian family to rear one right! At this writing, there are only four left on earth of the ten born to our parents. As I have so often said to my brothers and sisters, *the best family reunion will be when we are together with the Lord—in eternity!*

For anything done by our family while striving to say thank you to our Lord, may *all glory be given to God!*

Benson, Arizona—August 2008